NEO-PENTECOSTALISM:

A Sociological Assessment

Cecil David Bradfield
James Madison University

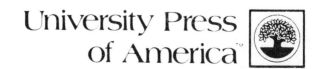

University Press
of America

TO

MY DAUGHTER

ANNE CECILIA BRADFIELD

PREFACE

The purpose of this monograph is to explore one of the most significant developments within American Christianity in this century. That development has been variously labeled as neo-Pentecostalism or the Charismatic Renewal. Pentecostalism began in this country around the turn of the century and until the 1960's was largely confined in its appeal to those of the lower socio-economic classes. Pentecostals were labeled as "holy rollers" and "sectarians" because of their intense emotional expression in worship which included the practice of "speaking in tongues".

Social scientists found that Pentecostalism was related to socio-economic deprivation. Pentecostalism, with its emphasis on the hereafter, was seen as distracting attention from the present deprived conditions. Further, with its emphasis on special spiritual gifts such as "speaking in tongues", it established an "alternate status system" to the one which existed in the larger society. The socio-economic deprivation perspective on Pentecostalism, however, was called into question in the 1960's as Pentecostal beliefs and practices emerged within the Catholic and mainline Protestant Churches with their predominantly middle class memberships.

Initially, the mainline churches responded with "alarm" to this "alien" and "sectarian" perspective in their midst. The early days of the movement were marked by conflict between the neo-Pentecostals and the regular members of the churches. The literature of the movement documents this era of "persecution". Conflict gave way to a series of studies in most major denominations. Today there exists more of an attitude of "live and let live" between the regular members and the neo-Pentecostals.

The study of neo-Pentecostalism is important because it may be indicative of what is happening with the middle class in general in contemporary American society. It represents a retreat, for example, from social activism. It is a response to de-personalization which has accompanied increasing technology and bureaucratization. It attempts to restore a sense of community in an increasingly individualized world. In short, it is an attempt to restore a way of life which is perceived as having been lost.

Neo-Pentecostals seek answers to their threatened situation within a religious framework. They have found their mainline churches lacking in meeting their needs and they turn to the neo-Pentecostal group. Mainline churches would do well to provide opportunities for their members to affirm themselves as human beings and to establish groups which will provide them types of affectionate interaction within the community of faith.

It should be noted that the explanation or the "cause" of a particular religious phenomenon will depend on the perspective of the respondent. For example, the "cause" of neo-Pentecostalism as seen by the participant is God. The social scientist, on the other hand, looks for "natural" causes rather than "supernatural." While I am both a Lutheran pastor and a sociologist the analysis offered is related to the latter role.

My interest in the subject of this investigation has emerged over a number of years as a pastor in Franklin, West Virginia; as a graduate student at The American University; and as a faculty member at James Madison University. The members of the Valley Chapter of The Full Gospel Businessmen's Fellowship International (FGBMFI) were most supportive of my efforts and without their cooperation this study could not have been completed. Many thanks to Juanita Swartz for her patient effort in typing the manuscript. Finally, my wife, Nancy, and my daughter, Anne Cecilia have in their own ways been a constant source of encouragement and love.

Bridgewater, Virginia   C. D. B.
June, 1979

CONTENTS

CHAPTER 1

INTRODUCTION AND RATIONALE

About 1955 neo-Pentecostalism emerged in the mainline denominations, and has had its most profound effect on the Episcopalian, Presbyterian, Lutheran, and Roman Catholic churches. Those Churches are farthest removed from Pentecostalism historically, doctrinally, and liturgically. The groups that have the most in common with Pentecostalism, such as the Holiness Churches, have been least effected.

Neo-Pentecostalism has brought into question prior sociological approaches to Pentecostalism which emphasized socio-economic deprivation. Neo-Pentecostalism has emerged among those who are not economically and/or socially deprived in the conventional sociological sense. The socio-economic approach to Pentecostalism was closely associated with traditional sect-church theory. In the sociological literature Pentecostalism was identified as sectarian and appealing primarily to the lower socio-economic classes of society.[1] Usually these groups were portrayed as breaking away from a more church-like group and then evolving into a denomination similar to the one against which they originally protested.

Neo-Pentecostalism, however, does not fit this pattern. It is true that neo-Pentecostalism involves such sectarian behavior as "speaking in tongues," "laying on of hands," and emotional expression in worship. But, neo-Pentecostals who engage in such behavior continue their affiliations with their mainline churches rather than breaking away in protest. Also, neo-Pentecostals are not economically or socially deprived; it is definitely a middle class movement. These considerations reveal the need for new or modified approaches to neo-Pentecostalism.

This investigation tests such a new approach by applying Charles Glock's theoretical framework of deprivation to neo-Pentecostalism.[2] Glock retains the concept of socio-economic deprivation as important for understanding the emergence of sectarian groups, but extends it beyond sect-church to include other types of non-objective deprivation. Glock's framework allows for the emergence of a sectarian response at any

1

socio-economic level, and so is most applicable to neo-Pentecostalism.

SOCIO-HISTORICAL DEVELOPMENT OF NEO-PENTECOSTALISM

For the purpose of this study it is important to indicate the linkage between the Holiness and classic Pentecostal movements and the neo-Pentecostal movement in America. Economic and social deprivation can be seen as important factors in the Holiness and classic Pentecostal movements. Neo-Pentecostalism developed, however, among those churches that have not traditionally attracted the economically or socially deprived relative to the society at large. This is a significant change for a movement that has been described as attracting only the poor and those of low status.

The Holiness Movement

The direct ancestor of the Pentecostal movement in the United States was the Holiness movement. The Holiness movement began as a reforming movement within the Methodist Church after the Civil War. Those in the group held three basic beliefs: the Bible was to be interpreted literally, each man must strive for a condition of moral perfection, and each man needed to experience a conversion experience and a second blessing. The major churches, caught up in the liberal trends of the era, rejected these concepts and so those in the movement separated from the parent churches and formed their own churches. The new group began to use revivalistic techniques and drew millions of people to the movement.

The Holiness churches developed a theology which stated that every Christian was to seek three blessings: conversion to Jesus Christ, sanctification and the 'baptism of burning love'. The concept of the third blessing prepared the way for the Pentecostal movement since the Holiness churches conceived it as being wholly personal--only the individual would know that it had occurred.

Thus, at the turn of the twentieth century in America, there was a resurgence of revivalism and the formation of a new and growing church group whose theology was based on the concept of an ultimate baptism experience in the Holy Spirit. The year 1901 was also

2

the first year of the decade in which immigration to
the United States was to reach its highest peak, and a
period in which great social changes were occurring.
So, there existed conditions of disorganization and
rootlessness which led people to seek certainty in revivalistic religions.[3]

Classic Pentecostalism

On the first day of the twentieth century, a young
woman in Topeka, Kansas, experienced the baptism in the
Holy Spirit which was evidenced by speaking in tongues.
This experience resulted from an intense study by a
group of Bible college students to find a certain sign
of Baptism in the Holy Spirit or the third blessing of
the Holiness churches. The Bible college had been
formed by Charles F. Parham, a former minister, who had
close ties to the Holiness movement. Parham's group
established the basic pentecostal premise that speaking
in tongues is an experience which invariably accompa-
nies the baptism in the Holy Spirit.

Between 1901 and 1905, Parham conducted a number
of revivals throughout Kansas, Missouri, and Texas in
which healing and tongues were experienced.   In
December, 1905, Parham moved to Houston, Texas, and
opened his second Bible school. It was from this
school that Parham's pentecostal beliefs were spread to
Azuza Street in Los Angeles. W. J. Seymour, one of
Parham's Houston students, transported Parham's beliefs
to the Azuza Street mission which became the source of
the popularization of Pentecostalism.

Pentecostal churches grew from the mission on
Azuza Street which "acted as the catalytic agent that
congealed tongue speaking into a fully defined
doctrine".[4] The new churches were usually interracial
and had similar doctrines, until 1914 when a general
council of all Pentecostal churches was called in Hot
Springs, Arkansas. The Hot Springs Convention formal-
ized a split in the Pentecostal movement on both racial
and doctrinal grounds.

After 1914, all Pentecostal churches agreed on
three basic beliefs: speaking in tongues is evidence
of the baptism of the Holy Spirit, tongue speaking is
the only experience necessary to obtain the full Christian life, and those who speak in tongues enter into
a "charismatic life."[5] Once a person has achieved a
"charismatic life", he is open to receive all the gifts

3

of the Holy Spirit, and he evidences a life based on love, compassion and brotherhood.

Between 1914 and 1920, the Pentecostal movement solidified its doctrinal and denominational stances. After 1920, the Pentecostal churches entered an era known within the movement as the "era of persecution." This persecution was primarily caused by the early enthusiasm which accompanied the rapid growth of Pentecostal churches. Since the 1920's, the history of classic Pentecostalism has been one of growing institutionalization. There have been no new major Pentecostal groups formed since 1932, and there have been no doctrinal splits since the late 1920's. Instead, the mainline Pentecostal churches have been involved in active missionary work, and in the building of colleges, seminaries and orphanages.[6]

Neo-Pentecostalism

Since the early 1950's, there has been a major new development in Pentecostal thought with the formation of Pentecostal prayer groups within the traditional Protestant and Catholic churches. The major differences between the "mainline" Pentecostal churches and the neo-Pentecostals is that the latter group does not require a member to speak publicly in tongues as proof of his Baptism, and the adherents of neo-Pentecostalism are encouraged to remain within their own churches.

The neo-Pentecostal movement also varies from the classic Pentecostal movement in that little or no effort has been made to organize the new groups beyond the local level. Each prayer group is encouraged to "go its own way and they make little effort to set up metropolitan, regional or national coordinating committees or councils."[7] This lack of national or regional organization has resulted in little reliable information on the programs, activities and size of the neo-Pentecostal movement.

Probably the earliest, the best known and the most representative neo-Pentecostal organization is the Full Gospel Businessmen's Fellowship International (FGBMFI). The FGBMFI was formed after the meeting of Demos Shakarian and Oral Roberts. Shakarian is a Pentecostal businessman of Armenian descent. By the early 1940's, he had weathered a number of business crises and was well established. He began to sponsor evangelism campaigns as his contribution to the growth of the kingdom of God.[8] It was while Shakarian was sponsoring these campaigns that he met Oral Roberts, a Pentecostal minister of national reputation.

In 1950, Shakarian sponsored one of Roberts' campaigns in Los Angeles. Shakarian told Roberts of his long-standing interest in uniting Pentecostal evangelizing efforts and in joining with other businessmen to support evangelical, Pentecostal crusades. Roberts encouraged Shakarian to form such a group, and in 1951, Shakarian gathered about two hundred Pentecostal businessmen at a meeting in Los Angeles. This group was enthusiastic and in 1952, the FGBMFI was formally incorporated and Shakarian was appointed president of the new organization. At this time, the men also formed an official magazine to spread the word of the organization, The Full Gospel Men's Voice.[9]

The FGBMFI met with little success until 1953 when Shakarian, disappointed by the slow progress, asked for a sign about his future and experienced a vision of men raising their hands to God.[10]

The original goal of the FGBMFI was twofold: to "stimulate fellowship among Pentecostal laymen",[11] and to spread word of the baptism of the Holy Spirit throughout the world.[12] These original goals were altered a little in the late 1950's when non-Pentecostals began to experience the baptism of the Holy Spirit. At that time, the FGBMFI added the goal of promoting neo-Pentecostalism. It has become the major promotional agency of the Pentecostal theology and experience among non-Pentecostals, and is generally recognized as being the most important and influential neo-Pentecostal organization in the world.[13]

Non-Pentecostals became familiar with the Pentecostal phenomenon of tongue speaking and healing through the television broadcasts of Oral Roberts, the growth of Pentecostal churches, and the spread of the FGBMFI.[14] The real beginnings of the neo-Pentecostal movement were centered in an Episcopalian parish in Van Nuys, California. It was in this parish that a mainline denomination minister, for the first time, sought converts for the baptism of the Holy Spirit.[15]

The Van Nuys experience began the introduction of Pentecostal prayer groups into mainline Protestant and Catholic churches. However, the spread of neo-Pentecostalism from Van Nuys was slow and vague. It is difficult to pinpoint with any historical accuracy the exact spread of the movement into various churches and denominations. However, this very vagueness is an indication of the character of the neo-Pentecostal movement. Pentecostal prayer groups would spread by a prominent person in a mainline church receiving the Baptism. The individual would start a prayer group and ask others to join. Thus, small and hidden clusters of neo-Pentecostals grew up almost unnoticed in the major mainline churches.

One of the major characteristics of the neo-Pentecostal movement is its hidden nature. There are no reliable figures on how many mainline Protestants and Catholics have experienced the Baptism and spoken in tongues. Neo-Pentecostals feel very strongly that they should avoid counting since they believe it stifles "openness and spontaneity".[16] Thus, these groups do not keep membership or attendance records. It has been estimated, however, that eleven per cent of the members of mainline churches have spoken in tongues, and that by the end of the twentieth century some two and one half million Americans will have spoken in tongues.[17]

THE RESEARCH PROBLEM AND THEORETICAL FRAMEWORK

The Research Problem

The research problem of the investigation was to examine the difference between classic Pentecostalism and neo-Pentecostalism, and to determine how these differences are related to the type of deprivation conceptualized by Glock.[18]

Prior sociological analyses of Pentecostalism have been generally conducted within the context of sect-church theory. This theory simply states that sectarian groups or movements begin as a protest against some organized group or groups. Initially, these new groups recruit primarily from among those who are economically and/or socially deprived. Over a period of time, the sect begins to take on the characteristics of the group against which it initially protested. Eventually, as this institutionalization process continues, the group becomes the source of a new protest and the formation of new sects.

6

One of the primary assumptions of this model, as applied to classic Pentecostalism, has been to associate its emergence with socio-economic deprivation.[19] While this approach appeared to be adequate for explaining the emergence of classic Pentecostalism, it is inadequate for explaining the emergence of neo-Pentecostalism. Therefore, new theoretical approaches are in order for the examination of neo-Pentecostalism.

Theoretical Framework

Glock's framework has been selected for testing in a search for additional factors not previously considered in sociological analyses of Pentecostalism. Glock was dissatisfied with a thesis which seemed to confine the dynamics of new religious groups or movements exclusively to the economically disinherited or the politically weak. Glock proposed an extension of these sources of strain to include not merely "absolute" disabilities or handicaps, such as economic and/or social deprivation, but also relative ones, such as psychic, ethical and organismic deprivation. These latter types of deprivation are not confined to those of lower socio-economic status. Thus, "religious needs" and "religious fervor" could theoretically emerge anywhere in the social structure. In this way, the investigation is an extension of sect-church theory as previously applied to Pentecostalism.[21]

Glock's theory distinguishes between five types of deprivation. The first type of deprivation is economic, which consists of limited income and access to the material necessities of life. It may be objectively defined and measured as well as subjectively experienced and perceived. Thus, although a person may not be technically poor, as categorized by some poverty level, he may perceive himself as poor. Such a perception can influence his behavior and attitude as much as or more than the objective facts of his existence.

The second type of deprivation is social. Social deprivation refers to the relative absence of such societal rewards as prestige, power, social status and the opportunity to participate in various activities and organizations. This is frequently a concomitant of economic deprivation in the sense that low economic status also means low prestige and respect, little power to influence others, and exclusion from much of the social and organizational life of the community. But, according to Glock, social deprivation is not strictly and necessarily correlated with economic deprivation. A person may be socially deprived yet economically solvent and successful. Social deprivation may be experienced by the old, the young, women or any group which may be economically established but which yields little power or prestige. Social deprivation turns people to a search for alternate sources of power, belonging and status.

A third type of deprivation is ethical. This refers to value conflicts between the ideals of society and those of individuals or groups. Ethical deprivation can also occur because some persons perceive incompatibilities in the values of society or because they are struck by the discrepancies between ideals and reality.

A fourth type of deprivation is psychic. Psychic deprivation occurs when persons find themselves without a meaningful system by which to organize and interpret their lives. A likely response to psychic deprivation is the search for new values, a new faith, a quest for meaning and purpose, and a search for closure and simplicity.

Finally, there is organismic deprivation. This refers to those who are, or perceive themselves to be, at a disadvantage to others in the society in the areas of physical and mental health.

Glock observed that the emergence of any protest group or movement, such as neo-Pentecostalism, requires some feeling of deprivation on the part of the participants.[21] They face a problem that is either not being addressed by the groups they are now affiliated with or is in some way produced by a group with which they are affiliated. Glock suggested that while some felt deprivation is a necessary condition for protest group formation it is not a sufficient condition. The deprivation must be shared with others, these people need to find one another, a leadership must emerge to suggest a solution or to organize the group around a proposed solution, and no alternative existing institutional arrangements or processes must appear to be available.[22]

RESEARCH DESIGN AND DATA GATHERING TECHNIQUES

Research Design

The basic research design of the investigation was a deviant case study contrasting Pentecostalism and neo-Pentecostalism. The study was designed to refine the understanding of Pentecostal, religious, and other social movements. As indicated above, there has been a very distinct emphasis associating Pentecostalism with lower socio-economic status and social disorganization in the sociological literature. Neo-Pentecostalism does not fit well within this framework as its adherents are not economically or socially deprived relative to society at large. Neither does social disorganization seem to be a strong factor in the sense indicated in the literature. Therefore, neo-Pentecostalism is a deviant case.

The case analyzed for this investigation was a neo-Pentecostal group in western Virginia. These neo-Pentecostals live in six rural counties and five independent cities with a combined population of three hundred thousand.[23] The FGBMFI, Valley Chapter serves as a catalytic group for the neo-Pentecostals in the area. There is no other group that brings the neo-Pentecostals in the area together on as wide a scale. Thus, the FGBMFI chapter in western Virginia served as the case for this study.

The FGBMFI, Valley Chapter, meets twice monthly with an average attendance of three hundred and twenty-five. Many of these participants have received the baptism of the Holy Spirit, others are seekers, and some are just curious. The participants are about equally male and female and represent a wide range of ages. The meetings consist of testimony, singing, prayer, special announcements and a speaker who gives his personal testimony. After the speaker concludes there is usually a special prayer meeting at which you "can give your heart to Jesus" or be "baptized in the Holy Spirit."

Data Gathering Techniques

The deviant case approach to sociological research lends itself to a number of data gathering techniques. This investigation involved the use of three techniques for data gathering: observation, a reading of the literature and a mail questionnaire.

Sociology is noted for a host of "one methodology"[24] studies in which a combination or "triangulation" of several types of data gathering procedures would have been preferable. While there are distinct advantages associated with each of the data gathering techniques, each also involves weaknesses that are eventually reflected in data deficiencies. The triangulation of method is a means of correcting such deficiencies.

Between September 1972 and March 1974, the investigator participated in the regular meetings of the group remaining quite anonymous among three to four hundred people. In March 1974, the investigator contacted the president of the FGBMFI, Valley Chapter, and told him of his interest in the group and managed to acquire the chapter's mailing list for the questionnaires.

An important part of this investigation has been a rather extensive reading of the in-movement literature and listening to numerous tape recordings of a personal testimony nature. These testimonies usually involve an account of what life was like before the experience and how it has been since the experience. Two magazines which were extensively read were Voice and New Covenant.

The literature used in this investigation has served several useful purposes. First, it provided background for the investigation. Secondly, the literature provided some of the themes that eventuated in seeing Glock's theoretical framework as potentially useful in understanding neo-Pentecostalism. Thirdly, it provided an important comparative source of data with observational and questionnaire data.

A third data gathering technique used for this investigation was mail questionnaires. The data gathered by this technique was inter-woven with the observation and in-movement literature data in the final analysis and interpretation. The final mail questionnaire list consisted of virtually every neo-Pentecostal who participates in the FGBMFI, Valley Chapter. While there is certain bias inherent in any pre-existent mailing list, securing nearly the entire list was a step in the direction of reducing the bias.[25]

One of the major disadvantages to a mail questionnaire is the problem of non-response. The problem stated succinctly is this--are persons who respond to mail questionnaires significantly different in ways relevant to the research problem from people who do not? The problem of non-response can be reduced by following proved procedures in the construction and mailing of the questionnaire.

A procedure which helps to deal with the assessment of the differences, if any, between respondents and non-respondents is to compare the first few respondents to the questionnaire with the last few respondents with the assumption being that those who respond last to a questionnaire are much like those who do not respond at all. The following table illustrates the difference in the first five respondents and the last five on the first mailing on the variable of education:

Table 1

Comparison of First Five and Last Five Respondents

Education: Median Years of School Completed

First five respondents --------------------- 17

Last five respondents --------------------- 13

This comparison would lend some credence to the assumption that non-respondents are less educated and are perhaps consequently less appreciative of the scientific method of inquiry. This consideration represents a bias in the data of this investigation toward the more successful and/or more educated. This bias is true also for the testimony literature. In a sense, however, this lends a modest degree of support to the assumption that if deprivation, as defined by Glock, exists among the more successful and educated, it probably exists to an even greater degree among those who are less successful and/or less educated.

CHAPTER II

DEPRIVATION AND NEO-PENTECOSTALISM

The purpose of this chapter is to present and interpret the data of this investigation related to the research problem of examining the differences between classic Pentecostalism and neo-Pentecostalism and to determine how these differences are related to the types of deprivation as conceptualized by Glock. While the analysis is structured by Glock's types of deprivation, in some instances it goes beyond them.

The chapter is divided into three parts: the deviant case aspects of neo-Pentecostalism as compared to classic Pentecostalism, other areas suggested by the framework, and conclusions relative to the framework. This investigation involves the triangulation of methods from the testimony literature of neo-Pentecostalism, observation of a chapter of the FGBMFI, and a mail questionnaire.

THE DEVIANT CASE ASPECTS OF NEO-PENTECOSTALISM

The purpose of this section of the chapter is to present and analyze the findings of this investigation relative to the differences between classic Pentecostalism and neo-Pentecostalism concerning sect-church theory, economic deprivation, and social deprivation. All of these areas have been important in prior sociological analyses of classic Pentecostalism and are also a part of Glock's framework.

Sect-Church Theory

Most of the theoretical approaches to classic Pentecostalism have been informed by sect-church theory. The review of the literature suggested that Pentecostal groups were almost always regarded as sectarian and also conformed to the pattern of evolving from a sect-like to a more church-like organization.[1] Pentecostal groups initially began as a protest against some religious group and then developed toward greater institutionalization. This has been noted historically as well as sociologically.[2]

13

Neo-Pentecostalism represents a reversal of this trend. Most neo-Pentecostals hold formal membership in those religious groups which are regarded as denominational or church-like rather than sectarian. It is this point that has brought a great deal of publicity to neo-Pentecostalism.[3]

The central religious experience of both classic Pentecostalism and neo-Pentecostalism is the phenomenon of glossolalia or speaking in tongues which has been regarded as a form of sectarian behavior. Therefore, neo-Pentecostals are engaging in a form of religious behavior distinctly regarded as sectarian and definitely at variance with the denominations in which they hold formal membership.

The findings of this investigation, as illustrated in Table 2, support the contention that neo-Pentecostals do hold membership in denominational or church-like groups; but, at the same time, they engage in behavior that is specifically associated with sect-like groups. The findings also illustrate that of the respondents who changed religious affiliation prior to the baptism in the Holy Spirit experience, the majority joined groups which were more church-like.

The general movement of the participants toward more church-like groups prior to the Baptism is somewhat supportive of sect-church theory. It could also be indicative of a general upward mobility of the group as a whole. It must also be noted that changes of religious affiliation often accompany marriage, and most of the respondents and participants in neo-Pentecostalism are married.

A distinct feature of neo-Pentecostalism is that while the participants engage in religious behavior which is definitely at variance with their religious group, they usually do not leave that group. Therefore, the participants are referred to as Pentecostal-Lutherans, Pentecostal-Presbyterians, Pentecostal-Methodists, etc. This does not mean, however, that they do not have dissatisfactions with the groups in which they hold formal membership.

Almost all of the respondents to the mail questionnaire indicated that there is something missing in the "mainline" churches in which they hold membership.

The description of what the respondents found missing
fell into two general categories.

Table 2

A Continuum of Present Formal Religious
Affiliation of Virginia Sample, FGBMFI

Church-like ----------------------------- Sect-like

	Catholic	Episcopal	Lutheran	Presbyterian	U. C. C.	United Methodist	Baptist	Church of Brethren	Mennonite	Pentecostal	
Percent	3	8	15	25	2	21	9	6	10	3	

Neo-Pentecostals who have changed
religious affiliation --------------------------- 45%

    Toward more church-like groups ------------- 60%

    Toward more sect-like groups --------------- 40%

N = 135

Source:

    Adapted from Liston Pope, <u>Millhands and Preachers</u>
(New Haven: Yale University Press, 1942), p. 124.

    The first type of response could be called the
"people are starving for spiritual food" approach.
Several responses illustrated this: A purchasing agent
said, "Mainline churches are becoming too Liberal, put-
ting too much emphasis on social action and not enough
on spiritual matters."[4] A pest control service owner
wrote: "People are looking for a better understanding
of the New Testament and the mainline preachers are
still teaching that just being good is all that is
really needed.[5] A homemaker, who formerly worked as a

15

nurse, asserted that: "People are looking for a living Christ who can change their lives and give them the power to become a person of worth, meaning, and in a right relationship with God."[6]

A second type of response in relation to what was perceived as missing in the mainline churches was the "form of godliness without power" approach. This could also be referred to as "the churches are merely playing games" approach. This represented a definite anti-institutional religious stance. This stance was often critical of ministers. A fifty-year-old high school teacher said: "People are becoming fed up with the game of playing church and listening to ministers who are trained by seminary professors who are personally unacquainted with Jesus as Lord of their lives."[7]

Another indication of anti-clericalism can be seen in the official position of the FGBMFI toward clergymen. While they may join the local chapters of the FGBMFI, clergymen are not permitted to hold any official positions on either the local or national level.

Church doctrine and tradition also came under such criticism as indicated by a Catholic homemaker: "I believe that most institutional churches have gotten away from the real Gospel of Jesus. They have a form of worship but deny the power. Too much church doctrine and tradition and not enough Gospel. Too socialized!"[8]

These responses indicated that there is a great deal of dissatisfaction on the part of neo-Pentecostals with the religious groups in which they hold formal membership. It is of importance to note, however, that this dissatisfaction has not led to mass defections from those groups.

The vast majority of the respondents to the questionnaire indicated that charismatic Christians should not form their own churches. They should stay in the churches where they hold membership even though in some cases they may be ostracized in those groups. The leaders of the FGBMFI openly discourage their members from leaving their religious groups. The Virginia Valley Chapter president consistently reminds the participants in the meetings that the FGBMFI is opposed to "church hopping" and also to the formation of new churches to accommodate only charismatics. Demos Shakarian, the International President of the FGBMFI, wrote on the topic of the formation of new churches:

16

> We [FGBMFI] never did, do we now, nor
> ever will advocate any man leaving his own
> church. The FGBMFI is not interested in
> starting new churches; rather we desire to
> be a service arm of existing ones.[9]

This article was apparently written in response to re-
ports that some teachers within the FGBMFI were advocating that neo-Pentecostals cancel their memberships
if their churches did not teach the baptism in the Holy
Spirit experience as held by the FGBMFI.

The major reason that the respondents gave for
staying in their respective churches was they they
should stay to witness about their Baptism experience
to others. A secondary reason given for not leaving
was so they would not be the cause of schisms. The
following responses were somewhat representative of the
reasons given for staying in the churches. A forty-
five year old Lutheran high school teacher said she is
staying in her denominational church because; "We have
a responsibility to remain with our people and demonstrate what Jesus can do and is doing in our lives."[10]
A Mennonite homemaker stated that while she wants to
stay in her church, she also desires fellowship with
other charismatics during the week. "I would like to
form a church that agrees with me. But this is not
God's way. He calls us to minister to those who do not
agree with us. I do believe that charismatic Christians need a strong body to relate to during the week
where this is not possible within the church."[11] A
forty-year-old Methodist dentist emphasized that charismatic Christians should stay in their churches so
that "they can be a yeast to influence others." He
attached a warning, however, when he said, "If no progress is made in the church, then a different approach
should be taken."[12] He did not indicate just what that
approach might be.

The desire to remain in their churches so that
they can influence others has often brought the charismatics into conflict with their fellow church members
who are non-charismatic. These members express the attitude that "the charismatics can stay, but they should
not attempt to influence the rest of us." The charismatics want to stay so that they can influence others
to their point of view.

There is some evidence that the level of conflict
is subsiding in most groups as a kind of "live and let

live" accommodation is being worked out. In many churches the charismatics are permitted to have their meetings under the auspices of the churches and in turn they "agree" not to interfere with the ongoing progress of the churches. This means that the charismatics may meet in the church building on Wednesday night and "speak in tongues," etc., but they would not be permitted to do this at the Sunday morning worship service.

On this type of limited evidence, it is the opinion of the investigator that generally the period of conflict is lessening in the churches between the charismatics and the non-charismatics. The general trend of the future seems to be toward an accomodation between them of the kind which has existed between liberals and conservatives in many churches in the past.

Many personal stories about this issue of conflict have been told at FGBMFI meetings. However, it is very rare for anyone to publicly criticize any religious group. One of the strongest taboos among neo-Pentecostals is "thou shall not publicly criticize any religious group." The triangulation of method, however, has made it possible to discern that what is not said publicly, may be said in private conversation and in written responses on questionnaires. Thus, the neo-Pentecostal has been confronted in the past with a basic dilemma as to whether he should stay in a religious group with which he has basic dissatisfaction. Many neo-Pentecostals have dealt with this dilemma by establishing their primary religious group affiliation with other charismatics while continuing a kind of secondary group affiliation with their mainline religious group.

Another area of concern in sect-church theory was the different levels of emotional expression in the sect as compared to the church. Churches tended to be more formal and lacking in outward emotional expression while sects tended to give free expression to emotions that caused them to be derogatorily named "holy rollers."

While most neo-Pentecostals have denied that they are excessive in their emotional expression, they have admitted in many cases that the experience has "released their emotions." It was not unusual for some of the participants to relate that the actual experience of the Baptism was the first time they had cried since childhood. While emotional expression was permitted

18

at the FGBMFI meetings, there were definite limitations placed on it. However, compared to the religious services of most mainline churches, a FGBMFI meeting would be regarded as very emotional.

In informal conversations with neo-Pentecostals they have indicated that, in their opinion, many middle class "church people" have been emotionally starved. That is, "church people" desire opportunities to express emotion without the fear of being frowned upon by their fellow church members. One never heard the question, "I wonder what is wrong with so and so?" when they were seen crying in a charismatic meeting. This would not be the case in most of the mainline churches.

In summary, the participants in neo-Pentecostalism were involved in some religious group prior to their Baptism experience. About half of them have changed religious affiliation prior to this experience. Of those who have changed, about three-fourths moved from sect-like groups to more church-like groups. Virtually all of the neo-Pentecostals in this investigation held formal membership in religious groups where the glossolalic experience does not normally occur. This fact highlights the contrast between classic Pentecostalism and neo-Pentecostalism. Neo-Pentecostals hold formal membership in more church-like groups but engage in behavior that is regarded as sectarian. This represents a reversal of the development of religious groups as described by sect-church theory.

While the neo-Pentecostals were dissatisfied with their religious groups, they were not dissatisfied enough to leave them or to make concerted efforts as a group to change them. The sectarian impulse to break away is present among neo-Pentecostals; but, as of this time, it has not caused a new religious group, which could entirely supplant the mainline churches, to emerge. Neo-Pentecostals hold two religious affiliations. One is with their mainline church which is of a secondary nature, and a second one of a primary nature with other neo-Pentecostals. Although the neo-Pentecostals do not belong to the same religious groups, they have the baptism in the Holy Spirit experience in common.

There is one final question that is of theoretical importance--why do neo-Pentecostals refrain from joining those groups such as the Assemblies of God, Church of God, and Pentecostal Holiness, where the experience of the baptism in the Holy Spirit is normative? Glock has suggested this as an alternative for a group such as the neo-Pentecostals. In recognizing that deprivation is not in itself sufficient cause for the origin of a social movement, he added that there is also required the additional condition "that deprivation be shared, that no alternative institutional arrangements for its alleviation be perceived, . . ."[13]

Why have neo-Pentecostals failed, in most cases, to perceive the above mentioned religious groups as a means of resolving their shared deprivation? The answer seems to lie in the consideration that while they share a similar religious experience with classic Pentecostals, they represent a higher socio-economic background. The decision to be a neo-Pentecostal rather than a classic Pentecostal permitted them to have the best of both the religious and the secular world.

Economic Deprivation

Another aspect of sect-church theory characterized sectarians as economically deprived. This was particularly noted in sociological investigations of classic Pentecostalism. Classic Pentecostals were seen as using the promise of riches in the hereafter to compensate for the lack of riches in this life.

It has been widely noted in the popular literature on neo-Pentecostalism that the movement has attracted people who are more affluent.[14] Oral Roberts has referred to the members and participants in the FGBMFI as God's "Ballroom Saints"--an obvious reference to their general affluency.[15] This relative affluency is indicated by Table 3 comparing the Virginia Valley sample and the U.S. Census data for 1974.

It must be noted that this type of comparison is based on objective deprivation as compared to felt or perceived deprivation. It must also be noted that the sample is probably skewed in the direction of the more affluent. However, it does indicate quite strongly that the majority of the respondents can be considered middle income when compared to classic Pentecostals who were regarded as being low income.

There is a marked contrast between classic Pentecostals and neo-Pentecostals in their attitudes toward wealth. Classic Pentecostals, who were regarded as low income, expressed the view that wealth tended to separate Christians from the things of God. They posited poverty in this life but riches in the next life. Neo-Pentecostals, who are regarded as being middle income and comparatively more affluent than classic Pentecostals, posited wealth in this life as well as in the after life. However, many neo-Pentecostals recognized the potential dangers of wealth in separating a Christian from the things of God.

Table 3

A Comparison of Family Income of Virginia Sample, FGBMFI and United States

Income Categories	Virginia Sample FGBMFI	U.S.
Below $10,000	7%	39%
$10,000 - $25.000	75%	52%
Over $25,000	18%	9%
	N = 135	

Source:

Column 3: U.S. Commerce and Treasury Depts., Securities and Exchange Commission, U.S. News and World Report, "Closer Look at the Middle Class," Vol. LXXVII (October 14, 1974), p. 41.

Only about one-fifth of the respondents to the questionnaire indicated the belief that wealth "almost always leads Christians away from the things of God." The other four-fifths believed that wealth, in fact, may bring a person closer to God rather than to separate him from God. It was always regarded as important that the individual be "Spirit-directed" rather than "self-directed" in the accumulation and use of his wealth. One of the leading teachers among neo-Pentecostals, in discussing the rich men of the Old Testament such as Abraham, stated: "It is time again, it is time once again for men of God to be the wealthiest men in the world. That time has come. Praise the Lord!"[16]

An example of testimony literature that emphasizes financial wealth as a result of the baptism in the Holy Spirit is "The Angelo Ferri Story" reported in the March, 1974, issue of <u>Voice</u>.[17] The story tells of the many illnesses and financial setbacks of Mr. Ferri who "finally found prosperity in obedience to the Word of God." Mr. Ferri says:

> Since 1969, our company, built upon faith and obedience to God's Word, has gone on to become the world's largest potato distributor, handling more frozen potatoes than the next eight largest companies combined. And very recently, God has enabled us to take over the whole steak program of the restaurant chain I do business with. . . . God's promise is for all. Material prosperity and wealth are His products for all who love and serve him.[18]

Many of the respondents to the questionnaire also believed that they had been helped financially as a direct result of the baptism in the Holy Spirit. Some of these respondents believed that they had been helped in a dramatic manner while others believed they had been helped in a more general way. The following statements represent some of the ways in which the respondents believe they were helped: A Baptist postmaster said: "I have had large sums of money pressed in my hand from spirit-filled Christians at just the right time. The Holy Spirit is the administrator of a very prosperous banking system in the kingdom on earth."[19] A Presbyterian salesman said: "Since being Baptized in the Holy Spirit my salary has doubled and we moved from a three bedroom house to a new five bedroom house."[20] A Catholic insurance agent spoke of the direct answer to prayer for financial help: "I prayed in the Spirit that I go to Israel, I asked for $700 and He sent me $1500."[21]

Although three-fourths of the respondents believed that they had been helped financially as a direct result of the Baptism, only about one-fifth of them sought the Baptism because of economic difficulties. Simply because people believe they have found something in an experience does not mean that they initially sought the experience on that basis.

The neo-Pentecostal attitude toward wealth is representative of a consistent theme that has emerged from this investigation. Neo-Pentecostals place

22

responsibility for their destiny outside themselves.
If one is financially successful, for instance, God is
responsible. One need not be uncomfortable if he hap-
pens to be wealthy because it is an indication of the
favor of God.

Neo-Pentecostalism, then, represents a definite
deviation from classic Pentecostalism in the area of
economic deprivation. The participants are more affluent than were participants in classic Pentecostalism. Consequently, perhaps, they also have a more
positive attitude toward wealth. They have integrated
wealth into their belief system by attributing it to
God rather than to themselves. If they have wealth, it
is usually taken as an unmistakable sign that God
favors it. Therefore, they are relieved of the conflict between financial success and their religious
values.

Social Deprivation

Social deprivation has been considered separately
from economic deprivation in this investigation for two
reasons. First, this procedure follows the theoretical
framework suggested by Glock; secondly, the economic
yardstick alone is not an accurate indicator of social
status. For example, in some areas of the country,
street cleaners and truck drivers may earn more than an
experienced high school teacher even though they would
have a lower social status. According to Glock:

> Social deprivation is based on society's
> propensity to value some attributes of indi-
> viduals and groups more highly than others and
> to distribute such rewards as prestige, power,
> status, and opportunities for social partici-
> pation accordingly. Social deprivation, then,
> arises out of the differential distribution of
> highly regarded attributes.[22]

Several areas of objective social deprivation considered were age, sex, education, occupation, and organizational memberships. Other areas considered are
of theoretical interest. These are an emphasis on
power, search for belonging, and an alternate status
system.

Age. Glock notes that in American society, youth
and old age constitute a kind of social deprivation because these are periods in the life cycle of relative

powerlessness. On this basis the respondents cannot be considered objectively socially deprived as the great majority of them are in the age ranges of twenty-five to fifty-four years as indicated by the following table:

Table 4

Age Distribution, Virginia Sample, FGBMFI

Age Categories	Virginia Sample, FGBMFI
20 - 24	6 per cent
25 - 34	27 per cent
35 - 44	25 per cent
45 - 54	30 per cent
55 - 61	4 per cent
62 - 74	5 per cent
75 and over	2 per cent
	100 per cent N = 135

The majority of the respondents, then, are in the "peak" years of productivity and social power. One possible interpretation of these findings, however, is the fact that it is during these peak years that males reach the upper limit of their occupational rise to power and that females are launching or about to launch their children only to find themselves facing the much publicized "identity crisis" of the middle-aged house-wife with its sudden paucity of purpose. This would suggest the search for an alternate system of values on the part of those who have found the limits of their material or social rewards.

Sex. Glock indicated that being female is a form of social deprivation in American society.[23] He also noted that there is a disproportionate share of women in most religious groups. On the basis of the data from this investigation, it has been found that the participants in the FGBMFI are equally divided between male and female. At first glance, this would tend to support the contention that there is no sex-related deprivation manifested in the group. A further consid-eration, however, needs to be made. While we are not able to determine with the research design whether sex-related deprivation led females into neo-Pentecostalism, it can be noted that they are accepting of a great deal of objective sex-related deprivation within the FGBMFI. Women are not permitted to speak in an official capacity in the meetings, they are not eligible for membership, and Voice magazine does not contain articles by or about women. Also, certain meetings are designated "for men only." The testimonies at the meetings and the testimony literature are consistent in emphasizing that where husband and wife relationships are concerned, the wife is to be subordinate to the husband.

Part of the acceptance of this objectively subordinate position is attributed to following the Biblical pattern of the recognized authority of the husband over the wife. From a sociological perspective, it may be inferred that female involvement in neo-Pentecostalism is related to the point made previously about the female "identity crisis" as the children are launched, the female begins seeking some alternative system of value.

Education. Lack of education has been widely regarded by sociologists as a form of deprivation in American society and as a strong causal factor in the emergence of sectarian groups such as Pentecostalism. The popular literature on neo-Pentecostalism has noted that the participants are not educationally deprived relative to American society. This observation is supported in Table 5.

Table 5

A Comparison of Median Years of School
Completed of Virginia Sample,
FGBMFI, Virginia, and U.S.

Virginia Sample, FGBMFI	Virginia Census, 1970	U.S. Census, 1970
14.5[a] N = 135	11.7	12.1

[a]Forty percent of Virginia Sample, FGBMFI, are college graduates.

These respondents cannot be considered educationally deprived. This assertion has to be tempered, however, with the consideration that the more educated are
more likely to respond to mail questionnaires. However, the high rate of return for the questionnaire
tends to reduce this problem.

Occupation. Occupation has been a primary indicator of social status, prestige, or power in American
society. In an effort to assess the relative occupational status of the respondents, a comparison was made
between the gross occupational categories of the sample
and the Virginia census.

Table 6

A Comparative Distribution of Gross
Occupational Categories:
Virginia Sample, FGBMFI,
and Virginia 1970 Census

Occupation[a]	Virginia Sample FGBMFI	Virginia Census 1970
Professional-Managerial	65%	28.5%
Clerical, Sales, and Kindred	35%	52.5%
Skilled and Unskilled Labor	0%	19.0%
	N = 101	

[a]Housewives are excluded from this table.

Source:

Column 1: Alba M. Edward, "Index: Social-economic
Grouping of Occupations" in Delbert C. Miller, Hand-
book of Research Design and Social Measurement (New
York: David McKay, Inc., 1970), pp. 170-171.

The above table indicates that in reference to
present occupation, the respondents are well above the
Virginia Census. Again, we are measuring absolute deprivation rather than relative deprivation.

An effort was also made in this investigation to assess occupational mobility. This was carried out by simply determining how many of the respondents were upwardly mobile in comparison to previous occupations and also in comparison to occupation of fathers. The following table illustrates the results:

Table 7

Occupational Mobility: A Comparison
of Present Occupation, Previous
Occupation, and Occupation of Father

Mobility	Previous Occupation[a]	Father's Occupation[a]
Upwardly Mobile	80%	90%
Downwardly Mobile	20%	10%
	N = 65	N = 83

[a]The above percentages necessarily omit respondents without previous occupations and those who did not answer the question.

Source:

"United States 1960 Socio-Economic Status Scores Index" in Delbert C. Miller, Handbook of Research Design and Social Measurement (New York: David McKay, Inc., 1970), pp. 178-193.

It can be noted from the above table that the neo-Pentecostal respondents are generally upwardly mobile in relation to previous occupations and in comparison to occupation of father. Two categories not indicated on this table are the present occupational designations of housewife and retired. About twenty-five per cent of the respondents were "housewives" and about eight per cent "retired." As already indicated, both of these designations represent a type of marginality in American society. The role of homemaker, however, is given credibility and support among neo-Pentecostals because it is perceived as fulfilling the God-given role for women. Retired persons find meaning, occupation, and purpose by carrying out the "requirements" of participation and meditation. The "ministry" of prayer, for example, is an important emphasis among neo-Pentecostals and one which can be carried out by the retired.

Organizational Membership. Another objective measure of social deprivation, according to Glock, is lack of organizational memberships.[24] He called this measure the Index of Organizational Involvement which specified the amount and degree of attachment to religious and/or secular organizations. The following table shows the degree of organizational involvement of the Virginia Valley Sample, FGBMFI. The table illustrates that more than three-fourths of the respondents hold membership in one or more organizations besides their religious affiliation. While it was not possible to assess the sample relative to the population, this finding is supportive of the deviant nature of neo-Pentecostalism relative to classic Pentecostalism. Liston Pope observed that classic Pentecostals usually belonged only to the religious sect or group.[25]

Table 8

Organizational Memberships,
Virginia Sample, FGBMFI

Organizational Memberships	Percentage of Virginia Sample
None besides church membership	22
At least one besides church membership	33
Two besides church membership	20
Three or more besides church membership	25
	N = 135

Another measure used to indicate type of organizational involvement is whether organizational involvement is primarily religious or secular. The procedure for this was simply to count the number of organizational memberships of a respondent including church membership and place them in three categories. Table 9 illustrates this procedure:

Table 9

Type of Organizational Involvement
of Virginia Sample, FGBMFI

Type of Organization	Percentage of Virginia Sample
More religious than secular	60
More secular than religious	16
Equally religious and secular	24
	N = 135

The table demonstrates that the respondents are oriented primarily toward religious types of organizations. Several respondents indicated what has been observed. Once participants become involved in the charismatic renewal, they tend to become inactive in secular organizations.[26] A high school teacher expressed this phenomenon when she said: "Since the baptism in the Holy Spirit I have become relatively inactive in the Ornithological Society, Home Demonstration Club, Fine Arts Club, Poetry Club and Kappa Delta Pi."[27]

Due to the research design of this investigation, it is difficult to make a highly refined analysis of what happened to organizational memberships before and after involvement in neo-Pentecostalism. Most of the data, therefore, is of a somewhat static nature. Some inferences, however, can be made.

It has been noted previously that neo-Pentecostals are persons who, even prior to their involvement in neo-Pentecostalism, had essentially a religious perspective and oriented their lives around their churches. Many of the religious organizations mentioned were directly related to their church membership such as women of the church, men of the church, missionary societies, etc. An apparent decline of interest in these church-related organizations may be accounted for by their dissatisfactions with their churches and that while they participate in the major worship services of these churches, they participate less in the "peripheral" organizations and refocus their efforts toward the neo-Pentecostal groups.

A more refined analysis of the non-religious affiliations by the respondents indicates that the most prominent affiliation was with service types of organizations like Lions, Kiwanis, Ruritans, Women's Clubs, Heart Fund, Cancer Society, etc. While such organizations take a kind of "band-aid" approach to problems, the apparent turning away from these organizations on the part of neo-Pentecostals may be an indication of the extent to which they have lost faith in human efforts to deal with human problems.

The neo-Pentecostal group supports the proposition that human efforts to deal with problems are futile and that these should be turned over to God for solution. This relieves the participants of the responsibility of dealing with the problems. Also, they are relieved of the conflict which may emerge as they consider their relatively privileged position in comparison to the disprivileged position of others.

Another factor which may be important in understanding the apparent refocusing of interest toward the neo-Pentecostal groups and away from other groups is that the charismatic experience is related to the totality of life whereas other groups are perceived to be segmental in character. This relates to the neo-Pentecostal emphasis on wholeness. In this sense, it may be inferred that neo-Pentecostalism represents a reaction against segmentation which they perceive in contemporary American life.

To deal more effectively with the important issue of organizational involvement, a different research procedure is needed of a longitudinal nature which could effectively deal with how involvement in neo-Pentecostalism has affected the degree and types of organizational involvement among neo-Pentecostals. It can be said, however, on the basis of this data that neo-Pentecostals are not deprived due to lack of organizational memberships of a religious or non-religious nature. In this sense they are deviant from classic

Pentecostals who were seen as belonging only to the religious group or sect and were excluded from other types of groups. Neo-Pentecostals appear to choose to refocus their affiliations, however, on the neo-Pentecostal group, and other affiliations seem to become less important.

Emphasis on Power. There has been a consistent emphasis among neo-Pentecostals on "power" as one of the manifestations of the Holy Spirit. It is not surprising, therefore, that almost all of the respondents indicated that they experienced a new power in their lives as a result of the baptism of the Holy Spirit. The description of this power was quite varied. Three categories were constructed for the responses: power to witness, power to overcome problems, and power to understand the power of God and His word.

The most common description of power was "power to witness to others about my faith." This is the "correct" scriptural answer as indicated by Acts 1:8. Approximately one-half of the respondents answered in this general category. A fifty-year-old Lutheran housewife, who spoke of her shyness before the Baptism, said that the experience gave her". . . a boldness to speak to others about Jesus and to share His love for them. A real concern for the lost and a compassion I never had before."[28]

A second description of this power was that it provided a means for overcoming the problems of life. About one-fourth of the respondents indicated that the Baptism gave them power to overcome problems that had beset them in the past. A forty-year-old air traffic control instructor said simply that "the power provided him with the means to live a 'life overcoming former problems'."[29]

A third description of the power of the Holy Spirit was more quietistic. This type of response indicated that the new power helped one to understand the reality of God and His word. About one-fourth of the respondents described the new power in this manner. A male Presbyterian school teacher stated that the new power gave him ". . . a greater comprehension of the scriptures (teaching takes a new vigor) . . . there seems to be a greater indwelling of peace and authority that is not particularly manifested outwardly."[30]

31

Sociological theorists, such as Bryan Wilson,[31] noted that classic Pentecostals emphasized "spiritual power" because they lacked social power. It can be argued that the "spiritual power" that neo-Pentecostals refer to has social implications. The power to "witness" is a very real power to influence others. The power of prayer to change personal, organizational, national and international situations is constantly cited. Healing power has obvious social benefits. One neo-Pentecostal put it this way, "You can get along without the Baptism, but it's like driving a car on six cylinders instead of eight."[32] It could be argued, then, that the desire for and receiving of "spiritual" power would be associated with relative and perceived lack of social power.

Search for Belonging. A regular theme in the literature on the contemporary American middle class is the "desire to belong," or a return to a more gemein-schaftlich way of life. Will Herberg noted this desire in American society in the 1950's when he stated that:

> . . . It is not difficult to see the current turn to religion and the church as . . . a reflection of the growing other directedness of our middle class culture . . . Being religious and joining a church is, under contemporary American conditions, a fundamental way of 'adjusting' and 'belonging' . . . . The trend toward religious identification . . . may thus to an extent be a reflection of the growing need for conformity and sociability. . . .[33]

There is a great deal of evidence among neo-Pentecostals of a strong sense of belonging. Neo-Pentecostal groups, large or small, promote close personal ties. Fellow participants are often addressed as "brother" or "sister." Physical touching is permitted between members of the same sex, and men are often seen hugging one another. Where it is at all possible, neo-Pentecostals sit or stand in circles, when they are involved in group activities, rather than in audience-oriented types of arrangements. When an individual is "being prayed for," hands are placed on that person's head emphasizing the personal touch.

The respondents to the questionnaire indicated by an overwhelming majority that they feel a "special sense of belonging" with other neo-Pentecostals as compared to Christians who do not share the charismatic experience. For example, a Lutheran neo-Pentecostal would probably prefer to be with a Catholic neo-Pentecostal rather than with a non-charismatic Lutheran.

Most of the respondents indicated that they felt a special sense of belonging with other charismatics because there was a deeper level of understanding and acceptance than with non-charismatics. A slightly different response could be characterized by the view that there is a special sense of closeness among charismatics, as well as a special interest. Both of these views are expressed by a fifty-year-old Episcopalian housewife:

> The Christians that I know without the Baptism do not even speak the same language-- what can we talk about--what can we do together that would have any meaning? If you are trying to be led by the Holy Spirit in all that you do, you do not have much in common with Christians whose lives are self-directed.[34]

A United Methodist elementary school teacher particularly emphasized that neo-Pentecostals are "my kind of people." She said, "I found my own kind of people in this group (FGBMFI). My whole hang up was not being understood--never feeling a part of the group I was working with daily. To me, they were only interested in themselves--I was never included.[35]

The belonging aspect of neo-Pentecostalism, therefore, is very evident. It is the promotion of this factor that has earned participants the label of being "clannish" and feeling that they are "better" than other Christians.

Alternate Status System. Sociologists such as Liston Pope,[36] in studying classic Pentecostalism, noted that it established an alternate status system to the society at large. Neo-Pentecostals are not deprived on most objective measures of socio-economic status. Despite this, however, neo-Pentecostals perceive the difference between themselves and other Christians largely in terms of seeing themselves as being "Spirit-directed" as compared to other Christians who are "self-directed."

Of theoretical importance at this point is Riessman's discussion of the adjusted, the anomic, and the autonomous man. The adjusted are those who conform to and at the same time make their peace with the demands of their culture whether it is tradition-directed, inner-directed, or other-directed. The anomic are those who are, in some serious way, shattered or broken by the culture; they are those who cannot, for whatever reason, meet the demands of the culture; they are lost to their culture. The autonomous are those who neither become lost in the demands of the culture nor broken by them. They live within the culture, but they retain a strong and assertive sense of self.[37]

Of the three types, neo-Pentecostals appear to be closest to the adjusted man. They do conform to their culture and make peace with its demands. They are not anomic in Riessman's sense since they are not shattered by their culture. They do not, as does the autonomous man, have a strong and assertive sense of self.

As a matter of fact, one of the strongest criticisms that neo-Pentecostals make toward non-charismatic Christians is that they are "self-directed." One of the highest compliments that can be paid to a neo-Pentecostal is to say that he or she is "Spirit-directed." This theme of locating the source of one's actions outside oneself is an interesting one that may be indicative of a sense of loss of control of their lives.

The respondents to the questionnaire were asked to give their opinions on the difference between charismatic Christians and non-charismatic Christians. The responses seem to fall into three general categories: charismatic Christians have a greater power to witness, a greater degree of Spirit direction, and a greater love and concern for others.

About one-fourth of the respondents characterized the difference as the charismatic Christian having more power to witness and live a victorious life and to overcome former problems. A general contractor said: "The charismatic has much more power--in witnessing, victorious living, understanding scriptures, etc."[38]

Another theme, mentioned above, characterizes charismatic Christians as being more Spirit-directed than non-charismatic Christians. A thirty-year-old Presbyterian writer describes the basic difference:

"The charismatic is led by the 'Spirit' and is 'spiritual'. The non-charismatic is 'self-directed' and is 'carnal'."[39]

Another one-fourth of the respondents indicated that charismatic Christians have a greater love and burden for others than non-charismatic Christians. A housewife characterized the difference in this fashion: "There is love for the Word of God, a love for Jesus and a love for each other; a burden for the lost and a real desire to serve God."[40]

Neo-Pentecostals are reluctant to say that they are better than other Christians even though their detractors say that they believe this. Yet they have had a religious experience that they regard as "higher" than other Christians, that is, the baptism in the Holy Spirit.

Another indicator of this superior place given to the Baptized is that the major officers of the Valley FGBMFI usually counsel with those seeking the Baptism while the lesser officers and board members counsel with those who are seeking a conversion experience or the "acceptance of Christ." Some neo-Pentecostals have attempted to deal with this problem by saying that "I don't think that I'm better than anyone else--I'm better than I was before I received the baptism in the Holy Spirit."

On the basis of this data it cannot be said that neo-Pentecostals seek to establish an alternate system of status to the society at large. They have not been excluded from secular society to the extent that classic Pentecostals were. Within the religous context, however, there is a kind of hierarchy with the "Spirit-filled" Christians in the top positions. It is this implicit hierarchy that has created a great deal of dissension between charismatic Christians and non-charismatic Christians.

The purpose of this section on social deprivation has been to look at certain objective measures of social status such as age, sex, education, occupation, and organization involvement. On these measures it can be said that the neo-Pentecostal respondents to this investigation are not objectively socially deprived relative to the American middle class.

There are, however, several themes that have been noted which have relevance for a greater understanding of the social origins of neo-Pentecostalism. Foremost among these is the desire for a more gemeinschaftlich way of life, a second is the desire or tendency to locate the source of one's actions outside oneself, and a desire for wholeness which is related to a desire for a more gemeinschaftlich way of life.

The general purpose of this first part of the analysis has been to demonstrate and explore the deviant case aspects of neo-Pentecostalism as compared and contrasted to classic Pentecostalism.

In reference to general sect-church theory, which Glock uses as a starting point in his theoretical framework, it has been noted in this investigation that while neo-Pentecostals do engage in behavior that may be regarded as sectarian, they hold formal membership in those religious groups that would be regarded as more denominational or church-like. Even though they have dissatisfactions with these religious groups, they choose to remain in them so as to be an influence. In short, neo-Pentecostalism represents a kind of reversal of the sect-church development predicted in sect-church theory. They appear to have their primary religious affiliation with other neo-Pentecostals and a kind of secondary religious affiliation with their denominational and church affiliations. In this manner, they maintain their social standing rather than becoming involved with groups which are compatible with their religious experience but not with their social experience.

In reference to economic deprivation, neo-Pentecostals are not deprived relative to the American middle class when objective measures are used. Classic Pentecostals were observed as being economically deprived and this deprivation was seen as a primary causal factor in the emergence of sectarian groups such as classic Pentecostalism.

Neo-Pentecostals who have some wealth have a more positive attitude about its possession than did classic Pentecostals who were economically deprived. Neo-Pentecostals regard themselves as economically successful, and they attribute this success to God.

Also, when objective measures in reference to social deprivation are used, neo-Pentecostals are not deprived in relation to the American middle class as was the case with classic Pentecostals. Neo-Pentecostals are successful occupationally; they are, for the most part, upwardly mobile; and, as with their wealth, they attribute their success to God--it is out of their hands.

On the basis of the available data, it has been demonstrated that on most measures of economic and social deprivation, neo-Pentecostals represent a deviant case from classic Pentecostals. While sect-church theory, with its emphasis on social and/or economic deprivation, was adequate to explain classic Pentecostalism, it can be seen that it is inadequate to explain neo-Pentecostalism. Other aspects of Glock's framework will be utilized as to their usefulness in understanding neo-Pentecostalism.

ETHICAL, PSYCHIC, AND ORGANISMIC DEPRIVATION

AND THEIR RELEVANCE FOR NEO-PENTECOSTALISM

Up to this point the analysis has focused on areas where neo-Pentecostalism is a deviant case from classic Pentecostalism as viewed within the context of sect-church theory. This analysis has demonstrated that neo-Pentecostalism did not originate in the manner predicted by sect-church theory as applied to classic Pentecostalism; also, neo-Pentecostalism did not originate among those who were economically and/or socially deprived as suggested by sect-church theory when applied to classic Pentecostalism. The analysis will now focus on other types of deprivation suggested by Glock's framework that may have relevance for a greater understanding of the emergence of neo-Pentecostalism among those who are not economically and/or socially deprived relative to the American middle class. These types are ethical, psychic, and organismic.

Ethical Deprivation

Ethical deprivation, according to Glock, refers to value conflicts between the ideals of society and those of individuals or groups. It can also occur because some people perceive incompatibilities in the values of society or because they are struck by the discrepencies between ideals and reality.[41] Following Glock's definition, it can be said that neo-Pentecostals are ethically deprived. The purpose of this section is to demonstrate this type of deprivation and its implications for understanding neo-Pentecostalism.

A great deal has been written in the popular press as well as in some sociological journals about the "squeeze" on the middle class and how middle class people feel threatened on one hand by liberals and radicals and on the other by Blacks and other minority groups.[42] The reaction to this perceived threat has been a swing to conservatism. Numerous attempts have been made to associate political and religious conservatism. After Robert Wuthnow reviewed the numerous attempts to make the correlation between the two, he said that the empirical evidence for the correlation was not strong.[43]

Keeping in mind Wuthnow's warning, it can be said, with a fair degree of confidence, that neo-Pentecostals are politically conservative. This is particularly true with participants in the FGBMFI. Observations of FGBMFI meetings over a period of two years would lead one to believe that the group as a whole is very patriotic. At the regional and national conventions of the FGBMFI there are scheduled "military prayer breakfasts" which feature the testimonies of military personnel who have experienced the baptism in the Holy Spirit. This may be a kind of sampling artifact because many of these conventions are held in areas of high military concentrations. However, entire issues of <u>Voice</u> magazine are devoted to the testimonies of military men.[44] Special booklets have been prepared by the FGBMFI to emphasize the testimonies of men in law enforcement, the military, medicine, and law.[45] These professions are generally regarded as conservative. Most of the respondents to the questionnaire also identified themselves as conservative. Table 10 demonstrates this.

In interpreting these results, it must be kept in mind that the terms liberal, moderate, and conservative, may be interpreted quite differently by individuals. Therefore, another measure was used in the questionnaire as an indicator of ethical deprivation. In short, what is wrong in American society?

Table 10

Political Self-Identification of
Virginia Sample, FGBMFI

Political Labels	Percentage of Virginia Sample, FGBMFI
Conservative	60
Moderate	36
Liberal	3
Other	1
	100% N = 135

The respondents were asked to list the three major problems in American society. For the purpose of coding this information, the responses were categorized as "two or more social," and "two or more spiritual or religious." Obviously, a few of the responses were difficult to categorize and arbitrary decisions were made as to their placement. The following table illustrates this procedure:

Table 11

Perception of Problems in American Society
by Virginia Sample, FGBMFI

Perception of Problems	Perception of Virginia Sample, FGBMFI
Two or more social (Crime, Lack of Honesty in Gov't., Inflation)	54
Two or more spiritual or religious (Other Gods, sin)	46
	100% N = 135

39

It follows the ideology of Pentecostalism in all of its forms that change should not and probably cannot be brought about by planned social action. This explains part of their general disenchantment with religious social action programs. The cause of social problems in American society is perceived to be individual sin rather than collective sin. Ultimately, following this perspective, all problems are spiritual or religious and the solution, therefore, must be the spiritual transformation of individuals.

It is understandable, then, that the respondents were almost unanimous in their opinion that the only solution to America's problems, whether perceived as social or spiritual, was in the realm of the spiritual. The solution was variously considered as "repentance," "return to God," "turning to Jesus," and "the baptism in the Holy Spirit."

While no specific question was asked about religious views in order to assess possible religious conservatism, it has been the observation of the investigator that most of the participants in the FGBMFI, male or female, tend to be religiously conservative. They are very orthodox on such issues as the Virgin Birth of Christ, the reality of miracles, the bodily resurrection of Christ from the dead, Christ's physical ascension into heaven, and His imminent return to the earth to "reign for a thousand years" during the so-called "millenium." It is during this millenial reign of Christ that all of the problems of mankind will be rectified. Most neo-Pentecostals believe the time for this reign is near.[46] This belief in the imminent return of Christ perhaps explains the lack of concerted social action programs coming out of neo-Pentecostalism.

It may be inferred from the data that neo-Pentecostals do have a sense of ethical deprivation as defined by Glock. The world is not as it should be, but neo-Pentecostals definitely do not feel that they are in control, even of their own lives. They are not inclined to make a concerted effort to change the world or to collectively address themselves to contemporary social problems. Their responsibility is to witness and bring people into a correct relationship with God, and to pray that God's will might be done among men. Men cannot solve their own problems. A retired Ph.D. summed up this view when he said: "Man cannot solve his own problems. Basic solutions can come only through DIVINE intervention."[47] A thirty-year-old housewife said, "I don't get involved in politics. I vote when I need to. I just sit back and watch the Bible come to pass."[48]

The growth of the charismatic movement roughly parallels a time of general unrest in American society beginning with the Civil Rights Movement of the 1950's and 1960's followed closely by the peace movement of the late 1960's. Almost all of the respondents experienced the Baptism after 1965. For many middle class Americans the Civil Rights Movement followed by the peace movement of the late 1960's were major turning points in their lives. These movements brought about an unprecedented questioning of dominant values and attitudes of American society, and presented the possibility of civil disobedience as a method of dissent.

Others in American society were, at this time, genuinely upset by the rapid pace of social change and the extent of the activists' dissent. This period of time was also a period of dissent and challenge within the church. It was a time when theologians were talking about the "death of God" and involvement in social action. Authority in all of its religious forms was being challenged. Many Protestants and Catholics felt the need for new authority to take the place of displaced authority, to tell them "where they stood," to give them assurance in the face of great change. Neo-Pentecostals tend to have something of a "crisis mentality" regarding the contemporary social and religious situations. Most of the respondents implied that in their view things are "worse" than they used to be. This negative evaluation of the present scene, however, is not too different from the evaluation of the general public.

Ethical deprivation, as defined by Glock, exists among neo-Pentecostals. They are disturbed by the discrepancies in the society at large, but they are particularly disturbed by the discrepancies within their mainline churches. Although it cannot be fully documented from the data of this investigation, most neo-Pentecostals are recruited from those religious groups which have been polarized between the "conservatives" and "liberals"--those who see the role of the church as "preaching the Gospel" and those who see the role of the church as being involved in "social action programs."

Neo-Pentecostals, to a strong degree, represent the "preaching the Gospel" approach. They believe that society can only be changed by God and through changed individuals. Direct efforts to address societal problems are futile. It seems that any full understanding of the emergence of neo-Pentecostalism in the mainline churches must take the polarization within them into consideration.

Ethical deprivation has been useful in helping to understand the neo-Pentecostals' attitude toward the society and toward their mainline churches. Their concern about the perceived disruption in the churches seems to be of significant value in understanding their involvement in neo-Pentecostalism. It is also a reminder that factors other than economic and/or social deprivation can be important factors for participation in sectarian religious beliefs and practices and, in this way, is a refinement of the concept of deprivation and sect-church theory as applied to Pentecostalism.

Psychic Deprivation

Psychic deprivation, according to Glock, occurs not in the face of value conflicts, but when people find themselves without a meaningful value system by which to organize and interpret their lives. A likely response to psychic deprivation is a search for new values, a new faith, a quest for meaning and purpose.[49] This is the type of deprivation most directly related to the meaning function of religion.

To apply the concept of psychic deprivation to neo-Pentecostals, it would be useful to summarize certain aspects of what has been noted about neo-Pentecostals in this investigation. Generally, it can be said that neo-Pentecostals have been successful by middle class American standards. They are relatively affluent, relatively well educated, and generally upwardly mobile. They have their reasonable share of status enhancing traits. In many cases they regarded themselves as happy prior to their Baptism experience. Subsequent to the Baptism, they regarded their former life as unhappy. Characteristic of this point of view is the testimony of Dr. Bob Jones, a member of the Indiana House of Representatives and an educational psychologist:

I thought I had everything. I was in my
third term in the legislature, had a lovely

42

wife, four handsome sons, a good business,
and prestige in the community. I was raised
in a Christian home, had been active in the
church, and thought I possessed everything
life had to offer.

What a fool I was! I didn't realize
what I'd been missing all of those years,
until July, 1971, when I received the
baptism in the Holy Spirit.[50]

The testimony of Dr. Jones points to one of the
"missing links" in deprivation approaches such as
Glock's to the understanding of why persons become involved in groups like neo-Pentecostalism. It was only
after his wife and several friends "witnessed" to him
over a period of time that he sought the Baptism. In
retrospect, he regarded his former life as unhappy.

This finding points to the need for research de-
signs of a before and after nature so that some accurate assessment can be made of the conditions which led
persons to seek the experience. Deprivation is an important ingredient in such understanding, but also important is the need to understand the dynamics and
ideology of the movement itself.

In applying the concept of psychic deprivation to
neo-Pentecostals, several sub-categories were used.
These were search for meaning and purpose in life, a
new self concept, the desire and search for closure and
simplicity, and attitude toward education in relation
to the experience of the baptism in the Holy Spirit.

Search for Meaning and Purpose. One of the popular themes in contemporary American society from the
youth culture to the aged is the search for meaning and
purpose in life. This search has traditionally taken
place within the context of religion, and some theorists see the "meaning and purpose" function of religion as primary to the understanding of religion.[51]

Glock asserts that people suffering from psychic
deprivation are the "seekers" in life.[52] Many of the
respondents to the questionnaire indicated that the
reason they initially sought the experience of the
Baptism was after a period of emptiness and searching.
A Methodist housewife expressed this view: "My life
was empty. I was searching. Then someone invited me

to a FGBMFI meeting. I knew from the very first meeting that this was what I was searching for."[53]

The terminology "being filled with the Spirit" commonly used among neo-Pentecostals illustrates this phenomenon. The following statements from respondents illustrate the search for meaning and purpose: "There was a parch dryness in my spiritual life--a longing to find the reality of God."[54] "I needed a purpose in my life, as a mother of three, and the wife of a wonderful husband, there was no real purpose--without the presence of the Holy Spirit in my life."[55] "My life was a complete wash out. I was on the verge of suicide. I was also physically ill. I knew that the baptism in the Holy Spirit was the only way that I could go on living."[56] "The only person I really loved, died. My life was completely empty."[57]

At least nine-tenths of the respondents indicated that the Baptism definitely gave them a "new sense of purpose and meaning." This must be assessed, however, rather cautiously as it could be a kind of "self-fulfilling prophecy" as in the case of "power." That is, since a Spirit-baptized Christian is supposed to find purpose and meaning, he finds it.

Over half of those who indicated that they received a new sense of purpose and meaning in life described their new purpose primarily as serving God through serving others. A dental hygienist expressed this point of view quite succinctly: "My new purpose is to live for Jesus, my husband, and others instead of me all of the way."[58] Many others described the new meaning and purpose as discovering God's will for their lives which did not necessarily involve serving others.

New Self Concept. Another indicator of psychic deprivation used in this investigation was a changed self-concept or new identity. Most of the testimony literature and the FGBMFI guest speakers followed the pattern of "this is the way I was before the baptism in the Holy Spirit, and this is the way I have been since."[59]

Almost all of the respondents indicated that as a result of the Baptism they looked at themselves in a new perspective. Some described the changed view of self as making them less concerned about their own interests and more concerned about God and His work. A controller for a manufacturing company exemplified

44

this type of change:

> Before the baptism of the Holy Spirit I
> was climbing a ladder of success, jealous of
> those ahead of me. Now I realize that my
> strength comes from God and He looks out for
> me. Success becomes easier for me and with-
> out walking over others. I am also more free
> to share my faith with others as my personal
> reputation is no longer the primary concern.[60]

This statement relates to the interesting view of success held by neo-Pentecostals. On the one hand they
are accepting of success; on the other, they are often
uncomfortable with the traditional means of achieving
it within American society. One way out of this dilemma is to attribute their success to an outside source--
God.

Of theoretical importance in this emphasis on success is Merton's means-end scheme.[61] Merton argued
that American society stresses the value of individual
attainment of success. At the same time the means of
achieving success are left mainly to the individual.
He elaborated further on this in his typology of modes
of individual adaptation.

Following Merton's typology, neo-Pentecostals, in
most instances, must be regarded as conformists. They
do not attempt to change the success goals of the society; and, they are following the institutionalized
means of achieving success through education, savings
and investments, and hard work. From their own perspective, the neo-Pentecostals attribute their success
not to themselves, but to God--an outside source. This
relieves them of some of the undesirable ramifications
of the means of achieving success in American society.

Most of the respondents indicated that the baptism
in the Holy Spirit helped them to look at themselves as
they really are and as God sees them. This point of
view is reflected by a fifty-year-old housewife: "I
am able to see myself as I really am. A sinner, lost,
but for the grace of God. My desire is to put God
first in everything: raising children, managing fi-
nances, relationships with others . . . everything. He
increases as I decrease."[62] Most of these statements
could be characterized as self-importance diminishing
responses. It follows the theology of Pentecostalism

that the "fuller" one becomes of the Spirit, the less important one is in his own right.

John Kildahl, in his psychological study of glossalalia, noted that almost all of neo-Pentecostal subjects experienced a sense of worthlessness before the experience of the Baptism. "Glossalalists reported that they felt they had nothing in themselves that was valuable or worthwhile, that they were empty, heavy, and powerless."[63]

For some of the respondents to the questionnaire, the Baptism gave them an enhanced view of themselves. An Episcopalian housewife emphasized that the experience helped her overcome feelings of inferiority and self condemnation:

> Most all inferiority feelings are gone
> and all self condemnation as the Lord has
> given me faith to believe His word about what
> I am in Christ. It is such a release and a
> joy to know what Christ has done for me and
> is doing--he will strengthen and establish
> me and is 100 per cent responsible for me.[64]

In many instances this new confidence has important secular implications. One neo-Pentecostal related that because of the Baptism he had greater confidence in himself; and, as a result of this new self confidence, he has been rapidly promoted in his company.

Thus, the Pentecostal experience seems to bring about important identity functions for individuals as has been noted by functional theorists of religion such as Thomas F. O'Dea. O'Dea wrote:

> Individuals, by their acceptance of the
> values involved in religion and the belief
> about human nature and destiny associated
> with them, develop important aspects of their
> own self understanding and self definition.
> Also, by participation in religious ritual
> and worship, they act out significant elements
> of their own identity. In these ways, religion
> affects individuals' understanding of who they
> are and what they are. . . . In periods of
> rapid social change and large scale social
> mobility, the contribution of religion to
> identity may become greatly enhanced.[65]

This new identity, whether it is self importance diminishing or self importance enhancing, for neo-Pentecostals is characterized by acceptance. The neo-Pentecostal sees himself as being accepted by God, as being accepted by fellow charismatics, and, as a consequence, he is able to accept himself. He is able to say in effect, "I am okay."

Search for Closure and Simplicity. Another aspect of psychic deprivation is the search for closure and simplicity. Most of the respondents indicated that they found life less complicated after the experience of the baptism in the Holy Spirit. This simplified life was realized by gradually turning everyday problems over to God. A flight training instructor indicated the extent to which he turned his problems over to God: "I now look at everything in a different light. God said that he would provide. I take him at his word and he does provide everything from financial needs to answers to technical problems."[66] The manager of a retail store stated simply that "you just ask God to help you and if you will listen to his directions, you will know what to do."[67] A retired air force officer said: "It's all in his hands now."[68]

The testimony literature of neo-Pentecostalism is replete with examples of men and women who have faced great tragedies such as deaths and serious injuries and still have found hope in God. The testimony of Henry W. Baxter, Jr., a Philadelphian, told of his son, Jonathan, who was a drug addict and died from an overdose:

> The name Jonathan means 'gift of God.'
> My wife and I feel that our son was indeed
> God's gift to us. Jonathan taught us many
> truths that we needed to know about the
> sensitive spirits of young people. He was
> a very loving boy, and we thank the Lord
> for the privilege of having him as long as
> we did.[69]

Even failure has been seen as a blessing in some instances. A Presbyterian minister reported at one of the testimony meetings of the FGBMFI that he suffered failure as a minister so that "God could get my attention." This failure was considered a blessing and the occasion for getting into another type of work "where God wanted me in the first place." Thus, failure, like success, is attributed to God. The individual is not responsible. This is another indication that the individual feels that he has lost control of his life.

The search for closure and simplicity among neo-Pentecostals is similar to a point of view noted by Arnold W. Green in Buchmanism or Moral Re-Armanent. Green noted:

> Buchmanism . . . affords a mental context whereby the complex becomes simple. It has made easily understandable the chaotic pattern of recent events. The blind march of power, crop failures, bank failures; . . . the disintegration of consensus and the claim and counterclaim of organized group upon organized group; race, class, and national hatreds --these magically disappear in a golden haze of rhetoric and good intentions.[70]

This statement represents one of many areas in which Moral Re-Armament and neo-Pentecostalism are quite similar. Among other areas of comparison, is the consideration that both movements appealed primarily to the affluent, fairly well educated middle class. This comparison should be pursued in further research.

Also related to this search for closure and simplicity among neo-Pentecostals is their attitude toward formal education. Classic Pentecostals were generally quite suspicious of education; and, it has been noted that classic Pentecostals, as a group, were not well educated. Neo-Pentecostals are relatively well educated but they are somewhat ambivalent in their views toward education. The respondents were about equally divided on whether they thought education was a hindrance to receiving the baptism in the Holy Spirit. Some of the more educated respondents like a Methodist minister who was previously an electrician explained why he sees education as a hindrance:

> Education is a hindrance because we tend to reason things out to our mind's satisfaction, and the connotations given to the 'baptism in the Holy Spirit' and 'speaking in tongues' cause any thought of the experience to be associated with the uneducated, emotional people in the lower socio-economic strata.[71]

A college graduate now working as a construction worker explains how education was a hindrance to him:

"I resumed my education because of Jesus but I was ex-
posed to such negative and critical books about Jesus
and the Bible that this has created a very skeptical
spirit within me."[72] A thirty-year-old art teacher explained why she thinks the educated person may have
greater difficulty with the experience:

> I feel intellect, a good mind which thinks
> methodically and logically, may have a more
> difficult time yielding to an unseen spirit.
> I have heard testimonies of that fact. I
> Corinthians 2:10-11 tells us God is revealed
> through the Spirit, not intellect.[73]

Many of the testimonies given at the Valley FGBMFI
over the past two years by persons with high academic
credentials have indicated that their education initially prevented them from having the experience. They
had attempted to explain the phenomenon psychologically,
theologically, or sociologically. In the end they were
overpowered and had the experience.

A Catholic educational psychologist related the
instance of his wife coming home and telling him that
she had experienced the Baptism. For a while he found
it rather amusing, then he became irritated, and finally he shook his wife physically and sat her "down on a
chair to tell her what was happening to her" from a
psychological perspective. Within a month after he had
attempted to explain the Baptism away as a form of
autohypnosis, he had the experience himself. Since
that time, he has been a widely sought speaker within
the charismatic renewal.

Slightly more than half of the respondents indicated that education need not be a hindrance to the
experience of the Baptism. A general contractor expressed this view: "Ignorance follows superstition . .
. . It is true that 'pride' is a hindrance. Also it
is true that 'faith as a little child' is a blessing.
Many a Phi Beta Kappa Ph.D. has that faith."[74] A
radio-television writer said: "God gave us our minds
and I am confident He intended us to use them to His
glory. The intellect sometimes appears to get in the
way, but that is true of the uneducated as well as the
educated."[75]

Despite a somewhat ambivalent attitude toward education and its relationship to receiving the Baptism,
people of high educational attainment are very

frequently selected as guest speakers at the Valley
Chapter of the FGBMFI. This attests to the value
placed on education as a mark of achievement.

Bryan Wilson, in reflecting the classic Pentecostal point of view about education, said: "Education
often leads a man to embrace the criteria of the world,
to embrace dangerous, heretical and intellectual conclusions of higher criticism and modernism."[76]

As compared to classic Pentecostals, neo-Pentecostals have a more positive attitude toward education.
At the same time, however, they view it as a potential
hindrance to initially receiving the "baptism in the
Holy Spirit." However, once the educated person over-
comes this initial hindrance, he is given a special
status among neo-Pentecostals attesting to the middle
class value placed on educational achievement.

Psychic deprivation, following Glock's definition,
seems to express itself among neo-Pentecostals in the
form of searching for meaning and purpose in life, a
new self concept, and search for closure and simplicity
with an ambivalent attitude toward intellectual pursuits.

Value conflict and ambiguity are not only conditions in secular society but also within the religious
groups in American society. The major conflict within
the mainline churches in recent years has been those
who advocate social action on the part of the churches
and those who advocate that the church "preach the
Gospel" to change individuals rather than to change
society at large. Most neo-Pentecostals would be
oriented toward the latter approach.

Dean Kelly, a religious sociologist, notes that
during the 1960's and into the 1970's the churches that
were growing in membership were those which were more
conservative and oriented toward "preaching the Gospel"
and relating to the meaning of life. The churches that
were emphasizing social action programs and involvement
in the ills of society suffered declines in membership.[77]

In summary, then, neo-Pentecostalism confronts the
problem of psychic deprivation, as defined by Glock, by
setting forth a deep spiritual experience that puts one
directly in touch with God. The Baptism gives a new
identity, it provides meaning and purpose in life, and

an experience and a relationship which provides closure and simplicity to life itself. If psychic deprivation is a condition of contemporary American life, then neo-Pentecostals believe that they have found an answer to it as they conceive it.

Organismic Deprivation

Organismic deprivation, according to Glock, "comprises ways in which persons are disadvantaged relative to others through physical or mental deformities, ill health or other such stigmatizing or disabling traits."[78] Healing, both physical and mental, is a regular emphasis in neo-Pentecostalism. Many of the written and spoken testimonies of the participants are stories of miraculous healing.

The neo-Pentecostal often views miraculous healing as a direct manifestation of the Holy Spirit. About eighty-five per cent of the respondents to the questionnaire said that they or someone close to them had experienced physical or mental healing as a direct manifestation of the Holy Spirit. About one-fourth of the respondents indicated that they directly sought the baptism in the Holy Spirit as the result of the need, on their part of someone close to them, for physical or mental healing. Parenthetically, this finding is a critique of Glock's functional approach. Even though a majority of the respondents believed they experienced healing as a direct manifestation of the baptism of the Holy Spirit, only a minority said they had actually sought the experience on that basis.

Related to the interest in physical and mental healing is the phenomenon of demon possession which is simply the belief that many physical and mental diseases are caused by individuals being possessed or inhabited by spirits influenced by Satan. Some of the members of the Virginia Valley Chapter, FGBMFI, are involved in the practice of exorcism. One of the men related to the investigator his view that about ninety per cent of all physical and mental illnesses are the result of demon possession. The respondents to the questionnaire agreed fully since about ninety per cent indicated the belief that demon possession is the cause of some physical and mental diseases. About three-fourths of the respondents said they knew of specific cases of demon possession.

This belief was previously thought to be confined to the uneducated and unscientific. However, the five respondents to the questionnaire, who identified themselves as medical doctors, all indicated that they believed in demon possession as the cause of many physical and mental diseases. They also indicated that they knew of specific cases.

The extent of the belief in demon possession was indicated at one of the meetings by a professor of education who is responsible for working with student teachers. He related that he recommended exorcism to student teachers who had very difficult children in the classroom. He reported that it worked in every case.

The belief in demons presents interesting, if obverse, support to the point made previously of the need on the part of neo-Pentecostals to locate the source of people's actions outside themselves. Neo-Pentecostals, it was noted, considered God the source of their actions. In the case of demon possession, the source of people's actions is attributed to Satan. This is an obvious contrast to the naturalistic world view.

Although the belief in miracles is somewhat at variance with the scientific world view posited by medical science and strongly supported by the educated middle class, neo-Pentecostals saw the possibility of the integration of medical science and a belief in the miraculous. Over half of the respondents to the questionnaire said that healings brought about by miraculous means and those brought about by medical science have the same source--God. The miraculous is different only in that it brings people closer to God.

About one-fourth of the respondents saw a significant difference in miraculous healing and medical healing; that is, miraculous healing heals the whole person--body, mind, and spirit. Others characterized miracles as taking place when medical science has done all it can.

The statement of a Presbyterian housewife was illustrative of the view of healing as coming from God: "God does all of the healing, whether by medical science or by laying on of hands. Neither is more acceptable or highly exalted. God chooses the method, I walk in obedience."[79] The holistic approach to healing was exemplified by the statement of another housewife who said simply: "When the soul heals, the whole person is healed physically, emotionally, and spiritually."[80] An Episcopalian librarian spoke of miracles as taking place usually when medical science has done all it can: "Miracles seem to take place when medicine has done all it knows how to do and can't do anymore."[81] A Presbyterian dentist, who had recently been healed of a detached retina, explained to the investigator what he believed to be central to the neo-Pentecostal understanding of healing. He said that man is a tripartite being--body, mind, and spirit. A medical doctor can cure the body, but the mind and spirit can still be sick. A psychiatrist can cure the mind, but the body or spirit can still be sick. Man relates to God through his spirit, and when the sick spirit is healed by God, the body and mind are also healed. Therefore, the emphasis is on healing the whole person. The existance of this attitude among neo-Pentecostals supports the theme noted previously in this analysis that neo-Pentecostals are reacting against segmentation and depersonalization in American society.

While most neo-Pentecostals do not openly derogate medical science, they certainly hold views that are at variance with those proposed by it. This does represent a rejection of a totally scientific view of the world at a time when there seems to be a growing general disenchantment with science and its potential for solving human problems. The belief in miraculous healing and demon possession represents a refusal to surrender to a purely scientific view of man.

There is little evidence that neo-Pentecostals perceive themselves as organismically deprived relative to others in the society. They do, however, have a great interest in the miraculous as it relates to physical healing and the need for such was the occasion for some persons becoming involved in neo-Pentecostalism. It is of interest to note that while healing was a part of the classic Pentecostal emphasis, it was seldom noted by sociological investigators.

One issue which has not been directly addressed in this analysis is that of "innovative leadership" which Glock sees as one of the conditions for the emergence of a new religious group. The FGBMFI has provided innovative leadership for the emergence of neo-Pentecostalism. It is the oldest and only neo-Pentecostal organization with an international network of local chapters which conduct monthly or bi-monthly meetings.

From the early years of its development the FGBMFI has
been ecumenical in character.

Also, from the beginning, it has provided a context in which middle class people could feel comfortable. The meetings are generally held in the better
hotel-motel facilities in a given area. The participants are well dressed, and a rather low-key evangelism
effort is mounted with an emphasis on person-to-person
witnessing. The speakers selected for the meetings are
persons regarded as successful in their work.

In summary, the FGBMFI has provided such leadership that it is possible to remain in a mainline denomination officially and at the same time engage in neo-
Pentecostal beliefs and practices in a context which
does not undermine one's middle class status. This
makes it unnescessary for neo-Pentecostals to associate
with classic Pentecostals who share their religious
perspective but who do not share their social status.
It is in this regard that the FGBMFI has, in a unique
way, provided "innovative leadership" for the emergence
of neo-Pentecostalism.

CONCLUSIONS RELATED TO GLOCK'S FRAMEWORK

The purpose of this section of the chapter is to
draw a number of conclusions related to the purpose and
the research problem of this investigation. The research problem of the investigation has been to examine
the differences between neo-Pentecostalism and classic
Pentecostalism and to determine how these differences
are related to Glock's conceptualizations of these
movements as "caused" by his types of deprivation.

It was noted that classic Pentecostalism conformed
to the dynamic pattern of development of religious
groups as predicted by sect-church theory. Neo-Pentecostalism, while having essentially the same religious
content as classic Pentecostalism, has not developed in
the pattern predicted by sect-church theory.

Sect-church theory also placed a heavy emphasis on
economic and/or social deprivation as "causal" for the
emergence of classic Pentecostalism. While there are
economic and/or social implications in neo-Pentecostalism, they are inadequate to explain its emergence among
those who are not objectively deprived on these measures

relative to the American middle class. It must be noted that this investigation has not adequately assessed relative economic and/or social deprivation. It may be inferred, however, that neo-Pentecostals do regard themselves as being of middle and upper socioeconomic status. In reference to sect-church theory, neo-Pentecostalism is a deviant case of classic Pentecostalism.

If the emergence of neo-Pentecostalism cannot be explained on the basis of economic and/or social deprivation, the deviant case analysis directs our attention to other factors suggested by Glock's framework. These factors are ethical, psychic, and organismic deprivation.

Ethical deprivation was helpful in pointing out that neo-Pentecostals perceive discrepencies between the way things are and the way they ought to be in both the society and in their churches. Neo-Pentecostals are greatly concerned with perceived disruption in society. They, along with the general public, think that things are worse now than at some time in the past. In this regard, they represent part of a conservative response in the society.

Even more than in society, neo-Pentecostals are concerned by the situation in their churches. This must be understood in the context that neo-Pentecostals generally are people who had a religious, church-related orientation to life even prior to the baptism in the Holy Spirit. Furthermore, they represent the "conservative" element in those churches which has become disenchanted with "social action" programs, "liberal" theology, and "secularization." In short, they express a sense that their social and religious world, as they have come to know it, is disintegrating.

Glock's concept of psychic deprivation was useful in pointing out the meaning element related to involvement in neo-Pentecostalism. It may be inferred that if persons perceive their social and religious world as disintegrating and already have an essentially religious orientation, they would look for a new or alternate meaning system in the religious context. Neo-Pentecostalism provides such an alternate meaning system which we might label as the "sacralization" of the whole of life. That is to say, a perspective which sees every aspect of life as related to ones' religion and interpreted in that context. This is in sharp

contrast to the "secularization" which they perceive
in their churches.

Glock's organismic deprivation has some relevance
for understanding neo-Pentecostalism per se, but does
not constitute one of the "causes" of the emergence of
neo-Pentecostalism or why people become involved in it.
It must be noted, however, that a few people did become
involved in neo-Pentecostalism because of the need for
healing, although the majority of the sample became
interested in the healing aspect only after involvement
in neo-Pentecostalism. It appears, then, that healing
is more a part of the ideology of neo-Pentecostalism
than it is a reason for becoming involved in it. The
concept is useful, however, in understanding the neo-
Pentecostal emphasis on wholeness and a kind of anti-
naturalistic approach to human beings. In short, there
is little evidence that neo-Pentecostals regard themselves as being organismically deprived relative to
other persons in the society.

This investigation provided a test of the usefulness and adequacy of Glock's framework for examining a
contemporary sectarian religious movement, that is,
neo-Pentecostalism. The method of investigation is a
deviant case study which is designed to refine our
understanding of Pentecostal movements and of other
religious or social movements.

The investigation has demonstrated that Pentecostalism, as a religious movement, can and has emerged
among those who are not objectively deprived economically or socially. Therefore, a religious movement
which appears to be related specifically to socio-
economic status at one point in time can emerge at
another time, under conditions of social change, among
those of a different socio-economic status. There
appears to be no necessary relationship between socio-
economic status and a particular religious perspective
as has often been assumed in the sociology of religion.

Glock's framework has also helped to demonstrate
that non-objective forms of deprivation such as psychic
and ethical, can be instrumental in the emergence of
sectarian movements like neo-Pentecostalism. Further,
it has often been assumed in deprivation approaches to
religious movements that individuals were deprived relative to some "outside" standard. An example of this
is to see lower class persons as deprived in relation
to middle class persons. In a sense, neo-Pentecostals

appear to be deprived relative to their own expectations rather than to some outside standard.

This investigation has also demonstrated that the capacity for the ecstatic in religion is not confined to those of lower socio-economic status. This has often been "taken for granted" in prior socio-economic status approaches to ecstatic religious practices and beliefs. Neo-Pentecostals, being primarily of middle socio-economic status, seem to be part of a growing appreciation of the "ecstatic" as a way of knowing.[82]

Deprivation approaches, such as Glock's, to the origin and development of new religious groups and movements tend to focus on factors "outside" them as "causal." What is needed to supplement this approach is to also focus on factors "inside" the group or movement such as its recruitment patterns. One such approach to social movements is that of Gerlach and Hine,[83] who emphasize five factors "inside" the movement which help to explain the growth and spread of a movement. These five factors are a reticulate-acephalous organization, fervent and convincing recruitment along pre-existent lines of significant social relationships, a commitment act or experience, a change-oriented or action-oriented ideology, and the perception of real or imagined opposition. Gerlach and Hine's implicit criticism of deprivation approaches to social movements was of those specifically emphasizing socio-economic deprivation such as sect-church theory as applied to classic Pentecostalism.

In fairness to Glock, it should be noted that he hints at "inside factors" of movements when he mentions the need for "innovative leadership." This is not developed, however, to a great extent within his framework.

One of the greatest difficulties with Glock's framework is its somewhat static nature. It does not adequately take into consideration factors related to social change and reactions to social change on the part of sectarians. To a great degree this lack may be due to the functionalist perspective which is not primarily concerned with social change but rather is concerned with social order and the conservative nature of religion within society. The following chapter attempts to deal with some of these social change related factors which have emerged in the investigation but which are not specifically related to Glock's types of deprivation.

CHAPTER III

BEYOND DEPRIVATION

Several themes have emerged in this investigation which are not specifically addressed by Glock's types of deprivation but which have relevance for an understanding of neo-Pentecostalism. From a sociological perspective it has been noted that sectarianism emerges in times of social change--usually rapid social change. Contemporary American society is in such a state of change that has adversely affected those of middle socio-economic status. Several areas of such change are noted in reference to those participating in neo-Pentecostalism.

Neo-Pentecostals are particularly concerned about the apparent disruption in the society at large. Their concern is expressed in the call for a return to "law and order" which involves a respect for authority. Ironically, some of the political leaders who were looked to for a restoration of such "law and order" were themselves found to be guilty of "unlawful" acts.

Education, which has been regarded by those of middle socio-economic status as a means of upward mobility and security, has now produced a surplus of labor in a host of career fields. Also, education has not provided answers to some of the great human problems as had been hoped. While neo-Pentecostals recognize educational achievement as a means of enhancing one's status, it is recognized that education alone cannot satisfy an individual's "deepest" needs.

Another area of change which has been perceived by neo-Pentecostals is the apparent disruption in the denominational churches in which they officially hold membership. While previously regarded as places of comfort and security "from the world," during the 1960's these churches became embroiled in the very controversies that were affecting the secular world. The controversy within these churches focused on the question of the role of the church in the secular world. Should the churches "preach the Gospel" to change individuals or should the churches become involved in "social action" to attempt to change the society? Neo-Pentecostals are solidly in the group advocating "preaching the Gospel" to change individuals rather than the church becoming "secularized."

59

Both as s concomitant and a consequence of these
and other changes traditional religious forms, answers,
and perceptions have for many become unsatisfying, even
empty and quite irrelevant. One consequence of such
perception has been individual and small group experi-
mentation with new religious forms, ideologies, and
structures. Neo-Pentecostalism is such a new religious
form which has emerged in an unsettled, changing,
social environment. Several themes noted in this investigation will be placed within this context.

One of the persistent observations of neo-Pentecostals is their success. On almost any measure of
success by average socio-economic standards, neo-Pentecostals are successful. Related to this success, however, is a certain amount of ambivalence. There is
evidence among neo-Pentecostals a "strain" toward success. The testimony literature and the questionnaire
data indicate that persons who experience the baptism
in the Holy Spirit almost always go on to be even more
successful than they had been previously. The emphasis
on success is evident, for example, in the speakers who
are selected for chapter meetings of the FGBMFI. Generally, the speakers are persons who are regarded as
successful in their business or profession.

As stated above, however, there is a certain
amount of ambivalence toward success in those areas
where there is a conflict with basic religious values.
Sometimes success involves "climbing over" other persons in a manner conflicting with basic religious
values like "being kind" and "loving" others. This
conflict is reduced or eliminated as one attributes his
success to God. If God is responsible, then the individual is not.

In classic Pentecostalism the making of money,
educational achievement. and occupational pursuits were
considered "worldly" or in sociological terms "secular."
These have been redefined by neo-Pentecostals as
"sacred" in the sense that they are attributed to God.
This is an indication of the extent to which neo-Pentecostals have "sacralized" the whole of life. This procedure provides them with a means of avoiding the conflicts that emerge within a competitive, bureaucratic
social system.

Another aspect of neo-Pentecostalism not specifically addressed by Glock's types of deprivation is the
implicit sense that people have lost control of their
way of life and of their own fate. Two specific

indications of this is the emphasis on "power" in conjunction with the charismatic experience and the tendency to locate the source of people's actions outside themselves.

Neo-Pentecostals, as did classic Pentecostals, emphasize "power" in conjunction with the baptism in the Holy Spirit. It has been noted by Bryan Wilson[1] and Liston Pope[2] that the emphasis on religious "power" is an indication of a lack of social "power". The power to witness, for example, is the power to influence other persons. "Power," like success, represents a point of ambivalence among neo-Pentecostals. On the one hand, power is necessary to succeed; on the other hand, the use of social power conflicts with basic Christian beliefs about humility. This conflict is resolved by delegating the source of "power" to the Holy Spirit.

Another indication of loss of control is the tendency among neo-Pentecostals to locate the source of people's actions outside themselves and attribute them either to God or to Satan. The highest compliment which can be paid to a neo-Pentecostal is to say that he is "Spirit-directed;" the most derogatory thing is to say that a person is "self-directed." Persons who commit "evil deeds" are often seen as being possessed or controlled by demons or Satan.

In this respect neo-Pentecostalism is one kind of reaction against the individualism which has a certain currency in American society which emphasizes "doing your own thing." It also appears to be a reaction against the Protestant ethic which places a great amount of responsibility on the individual for his own destiny. Neo-Pentecostals are interested in "getting themselves off their hands" as indicated by the following statement by a housewife:

> . . . It is such a relief and joy to know what Christ has done and is doing . . . and such a relief to have me off my hands and to know that he will strengthen and establish me and is 100 per cent responsible for me.[3]

The loss of control aspect of neo-Pentecostalism points to what may be an analytically efficient way to examine a social movement within a deprivation context. The procedure would involve focusing the analysis particularly on those areas where there is a congruence between a type of deprivation and the ideology of the movement. The emphasis on power and Spirit direction whould be two such areas in an analysis of neo-Pentecostalism.

Closely related to a sense of loss of control is a current of escapism among neo-Pentecostals. This escapism may be, in part, a reaction to a sense of having lost control of a traditional way of life. It could also be related to a sense of futility in connection with human efforts to solve complex problems in a bureaucratic social order.

Neo-Pentecostalism has emerged in American society during a time of challenge to basic middle class values such as law and order and the "rightness" of material success. These values are seen by neo-Pentecostals as being threatened. There is some evidence that they see their very way of life as disintegrating.

Another indication of escapism can be seen in the neo-Pentecostal approach to social problems. Neo-Pentecostals operate on the assumption that nations and institutions can be changed only as individuals are changed through religious conversion. This assumption enables neo-Pentecostals to transfer all problems to God and thus relieve the individual of social responsibility. There is very little "social consciousness" evident among neo-Pentecostals. This is one of the reasons why they are dissatisfied with "social action" programs in their host churches. Whether problems are seen as social or religious, the solution is almost always in the realm of the religious and "turning them over to God." In this manner, they are relieved of the great responsibility of dealing with complex personal and social problems. This point of view permits neo-Pentecostals to be comfortable in their way of life which includes success and material comfort without being confronted with problems which may tend to make them uncomfortable with their success and material comforts.

Another emphasis among neo-Pentecostals is an apparent reaction to the depersonalization and segmentation found in contemporary American society. In such a bureaucratic social order, where rationalization exists to an advanced degree, individuals are treated as "things" rather than "persons". Neo-Pentecostals are confronted with this orientation in the technical and professional fields in which they are largely employed.

One indicator of the rejection of such an orientation is the view of the miraculous among neo-Pentecostals. There is little, if any, room in a totally rationalized system for the miraculous. Yet neo-Pentecostals see diseases as being caused by demon possession and cures for those diseases as coming from God. This represents the extremity of the rejection of a totally rationalized view of man which sees him as segmented and depersonalized.

Neo-Pentecostals emphasize personhood and wholeness. This is indicated, for instance, in the typical comparison of "warm, personal" relationships in the charismatic group in comparison to the "cold, formal" relationships in the host churches. Even the more sophisticated neo-Pentecostals address one another as "brother" and "sister." The emphasis on wholeness is particularly evident in the area of healing which involves the "whole" person rather than segmented parts of the person. This can also be noted in the decline of interest in groups which are perceived as being "segmental" in character such as special interest groups and service clubs. The neo-Pentecostal group, in contrast, is characterized by interpersonal warmth, openness, trust, and emotional support which relate to the "whole" person.

From a sociological perspective, this escapism and search for wholeness may be facets of a pseudo retreat from a competitive, secular, bureaucratized existence. There is no overt attempt to change that system or to give up the advantages of work, success, comfortable living, socio-economic status, or the mainline church membership. The neo-Pentecostal group supports this point of view.

Thomas F. O'Dea[4] has emphasized the importance of the religious community for the sustenance of religious commitment. He observed that strong religious commitment needs the intense community of faith for its sustenance. Neo-Pentecostal groups, which are characterized by enthusiasm and emotional release, are capable of eliciting from the participants a spirit of unity. The intense life of the group exalts the personality, the participant in neo-Pentecostalism is caught in a kind of inevitable enthusiasm and release of emotions. This gives the individual a feeling of participation and consequently of strength and worth.

The "search for community" is not unique to middle class neo-Pentecostals. Observers of the American scene such as David Riessman[5] and Will Herberg[6] have noted this search previously among middle class Americans. However, the neo-Pentecostals search for this community within the context of religion. It has been noted in this investigation that neo-Pentecostals had a rather strong religious orientation prior to their involvement in neo-Pentecostalism.

It has been found on the basis of the data for this investigation that neo-Pentecostals have a strong sense of "belonging" with other neo-Pentecostals that they do not have with non-charismatic Christians. Once again, this "belonging" aspect represents a strong sense of community.

It needs to be emphasized that the community which neo-Pentecostals seek goes beyond narrow denominational or regional boundaries. That is to say that while neo-Pentecostals get together in a given location, their feeling of fellowship and community goes beyond these spatial boundaries; it is a kind of community sentiment. There appears to be several elements in this community sentiment. The first, already alluded to, is a strong "we" feeling in which each person feels he is a member of the group. A second is that each participant feels that he has a role to play in the group. A third element is a feeling of dependency on the group.

On the basis of the data of this investigation there definitely is a strong "we" feeling among neo-Pentecostals. Being a neo-Pentecostal or charismatic is very much a part of self-identification. Even females, who cannot officially join the FGBMFI, often indicated on the questionnaire that they were members. Non-charismatics are clearly identified as "not one of us." Neo-Pentecostal meetings are regarded as common enterprises where all are encouraged to pray for the meeting and the speakers. Persons are identified on a first name basis and there is generally a real conviction of membership in a brotherhood or fellowship which crosses denominational and regional barriers--a feat that the Christian Ecumenical movement has not been able to accomplish in approximately twenty-five years of effort.

A second element of the "community sentiment" among neo-Pentecostals is that each participant feels that he has a role to play in the group. Individual participants often have an opportunity to speak at the meetings, to give their testimony, and to report healing or other answered prayers. There is a strong emphasis on each charismatic as being a minister. The extent of this view is exemplified by the middle-aged woman who announced at one of the meetings that God had given her a ministry to "middle-aged women who are depressed."

A third element of community sentiment is a feeling of dependency. Each participant in neo-Pentecostalism knows that he is a member of the group, but he also knows that he needs the group to sustain his "baptism in the Holy Spirit" experience. This dependency is felt, for example, when the leader of the meeting calls for the names of those who are sick or in any other need. Neo-Pentecostals have a strong expressed need for the charismatic group. This dependency is illustrated by the following example. A woman reported at one of the FGBMFI meetings that she experienced the Baptism while away from home and when she returned home she could not find anyone who shared her experience. She described her dilemma as "starving to death" for fellowship. This is a common phrase among neo-Pentecostals to describe isolation from one another.

Another form of community found among Pentecostals resembles the "Gemeinschaft of mind" noted by Ferdinand Tonnies.[7] This type of community is characterized by "co-operation and co-ordinated action for a common goal." Even though neo-Pentecostals are removed physically from one another, they share a form of community so intense that there are few, if any, neo-Pentecostals who are strangers to other neo-Pentecostals. An executive secretary at a local college illustrates this "community of mind" which is shared:

> I feel very close to other Christians,
> especially the ones who have the baptism. A
> stranger can walk through the door, one who
> has the baptism, and many times both will
> recognize the other as 'one of us', a brother
> or sister in Christ. I have had this experi-
> ence many times, of 'just knowing' the other.
> Upon asking the question, 'You have the bap-
> tism in the Holy Spirit, don't you?' the
> answer is 'Yes, you do too, don't you?' We
> are becoming One in the Spirit.[8]

It appears that neo-Pentecostals are seeking a type of existence that gives security, personhood, and community and which makes all of life sacred.

Neo-Pentecostalism is one way of seeking such meaning and belonging. Individuals perceiving similar situations in the society and in their mainline churches are engaging in a collective enterprise and producing charismatically filled experiences, relationships and structures, that is, neo-Pentecostalism.

What of the future of neo-Pentecostalism? Will it eventually result in a new donomination, or will it be integrated into present religious structures? Sectarianism has followed both patterns in the past. During the Middle Ages, the Catholic Church was able to integrate the sectarians within the structure through the religious orders. Classic Pentecostalism, however, broke away from the parent groups in protest and formed new religious groups.

Any prediction about neo-Pentecostalism must be made somewhat cautiously at this point. There is, however, some preliminary evidence that neo-Pentecostalism will follow the pattern of remaining within the host groups rather than breaking away to form a new denomination. It is significant that over the past ten to fifteen years the host groups have become more tolerant of neo-Pentecostalism. At first, clergymen and congregations which were involved were censured. For the most part, at the present time, there is a rather high degree of tolerance. In a sense, this growing tolerance undermines one of the sources of growth for charismatic groups. Gerlach and Hine found that among important growth factors in such groups as the existence of a "psychology of persecution." Ridicule, non-acceptance, and rejection by traditional denominational churches served to stimulate growth, whereas, in those instances where local denominational officials did not oppose the movement, recruitment was more difficult.[9]

Why are the mainline churches being relatively tolerant of neo-Pentecostalism? Normally, such activity would be resisted because it is by definition beyond the control of the host organizations and is a challenge to traditional, organizationally legitimated authority. One explanation of the relative tolerance of the movement on the part of the denominations is that most people within the movement insist that they are not out to destroy or leave the organized churches. They rather desire to offer an internal, optional, form of religious experience and worship; they simply desire to enrich what organized religion already has to offer.

SOURCE NOTES

Chapter 1

[1]Anton J. Boisen, "Economic Distress and Religious Experience: A Study of the Holy Rollers," Psychiatry, 2, May 1939, pp. 185-194; see also John Holt, "Holiness Religion: Cultural Shock and Social Reorganization." American Sociological Review, 5, October 1940, pp. 740-747; Russell Dynes, "Church-Sect Typology and Socio-Economic Status," American Sociological Review, 49, October 1955, pp. 555-560; H. Richard Niebuhr, "The Churches of the Disinherited." The Social Sources of Denominationalism, H. Richard Niebuhr. New York: Henry Holt and Company, 1929, pp. 198-215; Liston Pope, Mill-hands and Preachers. New Haven: Yale University Press, 1942.

[2]Charles Y. Glock, "On the Role of Deprivation in in the Origin and Evolution of Religious Groups," Religion in Sociological Perspective, ed. Charles Y. Glock. Belmont, California: Wadsworth Publishing Company, 1973, p. 212.

[3]Kilian McDonnell, "Holy Spirit and Pentecostalism," Commonweal, 89, November 8, 1968, p. 198.

[4]Vinson Synan, The Holiness-Pentecostal Movement. Grand Rapids, Mi.: Wm. B. Erdmans Publishing Company, 1971, p. 115.

[5]Morton Kelsey, Tongue Speaking: An Experiment in Spiritual Experience. Garden City, N.Y.: Doubleday and Company, 1964, pp. 78-79.

[6]Synan, op. cit., p. 222.

[7]Erling, Jorstad, ed., The Holy Spirit in Today's Church, New York, N.Y.: Abingdon Press, 1973, p. 20.

[8]Walter Hollenweger, The Pentecostals. Minneapolis, Minn.: Augsburg Publishing House, 1969, p. 6.

[9]William Menzies, Anointed to Serve: The Story of the Assemblies of God. Springfield, Missouri: Gospel Publishing House, 1971, p. 337.

[10]Steve Durasoff, Bright Wind of the Spirit. Englewood Cliffs: Prentice Hall, Inc., 1972, p. 148.

[11]Menzies, _op. cit_, p. 338.

[12]Hollenweger, _op. cit._, p. 6.

[13]_Ibid._, p. 7.

[14]_Ibid._, p. 6.

[15]Jorstad, _op. cit._, p. 18.

[16]_Ibid._, p. 20.

[17]Weston E. Mills, "Glossalalia-Christianity's 'Counter-culture' Amidst a Silent Majority," _The Christian Century_, 89, September 27, 1972, pp. 949-950.

[18]Glock, _op. cit_.

[19]See footnote number one.

[20]See footnote number two. Glock's formulation is very similar to Aberle's in David Aberle, "A Note on Relative Deprivation Theory as Applied to Millenarian and Other Cult Movements," in _Reader in Comparative Religion_, eds., W.A. Dessa and E.Z. Vogt. New York: Harper and Row, 1965.

[21]Glock, _op. cit_, p. 212.

[22]_Ibid._, p. 210.

[23]U.S. Bureau of the Census, _Virginia: General Population Characteristics: 1970_. Washington: Government Printing Office, 1971, pp. 5-22.

[24]William F. Whyte, _Toward an Integrated Approach for Research on Organizational Behavior_, Industrial and Labor Relations Reprint Series no. 155. Ithaca, N.Y.: Cornell University, 1965.

[25]For more detailed information on the data gathering techniques see: Cecil D. Bradfield, "An Investigation of Neo-Pentecostalism" (unpublished Doctoral thesis). American University, Washington, D.C. 1975, pp. 89-113.

Chapter II

[1]Anton J. Boisen, "Economic Distress and Religious Experience: A Study of the Holy Rollers," _Psychiatry_ 2 (May, 1939), pp. 185-194; see also John Holt, "Holiness Religion: Cultural Shock and Social Reorganization," _American Sociological Review_ 5 (October, 1940), pp. 740-747; Russell R. Dynes, "Church-Sect Typology and Socio-Economic Status," _American Sociological Review_ 49 (October, 1955), pp. 555-560; H. Richard Niebuhr, "The Churches of the Disinherited," in _The Social Sources of Denominationalism_, by H. Richard Niebuhr (New York: Henry Holt and Co., 1929), pp. 198-215; Liston Pope, _Millhands and Preachers_ (New Haven: Yale University Press, 1942).

[2]Vinson Synan, _The Holiness-Pentecostal Movement_ (Grand Rapids, Michigan: Wm. B. Eerdmans Publishing Co., 1971), p. 223.

[3]William Willoughby, "Tongue Speaking Gains Prestige," Logos 4:2 (March-April, 1974), p. 2.

[4]Respondent No. 26.

[5]Respondent No. 62.

[6]Respondent No. 98.

[7]Respondent No. 83.

[8]Respondent No. 82.

[9]Demos Shakarian, "We Are Not Interested in Starting New Churches," _Voice_ 22:10 (November, 1974), pp. 29-30.

[10]Respondent No. 83.

[11]Respondent No. 98.

[12]Respondent No. 92.

[13]Charles Y. Glock, "On the Role of Deprivation in the Origin and Evolution of Religious Groups." _Religion in Sociological Perspective_, ed. Charles Y. Glock (Belmont, California: Wadsworth Publishing Co., 1973), p. 212.

[14]Willoughby, op. cit.

[15]"Photo Story: The 1974 FGBMFI World Convention," Voice 22:10 (November, 1974), p. 19.

[16]Kenneth Copeland, "Laws of Prosperity," Treasures on Tape No. 61 (Fort Worth, Texas: Kenneth Copeland Publications, 1974); see also No. 64, "Forms of Depositing in Your Heavenly Account."

[17]Angelo C. Ferri, "Prosperity is a Product," Voice 22:3 (March, 1974), pp. 2-7, 16-17.

[18]Ibid, p. 17.

[19]Respondent No. 29.

[20]Respondent No. 72.

[21]Respondent No. 6.

[22]Glock, op. cit., pp. 211-212.

[23]Ibid., p. 212.

[24]Charles Y. Glock, Benjamin Ringer, and Earl Babbie, To Comfort and to Challenge (Berkeley, Calif.: University of California Press, 1967), pp. 23-24.

[25]Pope, op, cit., pp. 136-137.

[26]This finding relates to that of Russell Dynes, that persons who had more sectarian beliefs and practices tended to be less involved in secular organizations than persons engaging in non-sectarian beliefs and practices. Russell Dynes, "The Consequence of Sectarianism for Social Participation," Social Forces 35 (May, 1957), pp. 331-334.

[27]Respondent No. 14.

[28]Respondent No. 36.

[29]Respondent No. 54.

[30]Respondent No. 38.

[31]Bryan Wilson, Religious Sects (New York: McGraw-Hill, 1970).

[32]Respondent No. 50.

[33]Will Herberg, Protestant, Catholic and Jew (New York, Doubleday and Co., 1956), pp. 72-73.

[34]Respondent No. 55.

[35]Respondent No. 130.

[36]Pope, op. cit., p. 138.

[37]David Riessman, Nathan Glazer, and Reuel Denney, The Lonely Crowd: A Study in the Changing American Character (New Haven: Yale University Press, 1961), pp. 246-259.

[38]Respondent No. 35.

[39]Respondent No. 109.

[40]Respondent No. 11.

[41]Glock, op. cit., p. 211.

[42]"Squeeze on America's Middle Class," U. S. News and World Report Vol. LXXVII:19 (October 14, 1974), pp. 42-44.

[43]Robert Wuthnow, "Religious Committment and Conservatism: In Search of an Elusive Relationship," Religion in Sociological Perspective, ed. Charles Y. Glock (Belmont, California: Wadsworth Publishing Co., 1973), pp. 117-132.

[44]See, for example, Voice 21:7 (July-August, 1973).

[45]See, for example, God and the Lawman, Voices of the Military, Physicians Examine the Baptism of the Holy Spirit, Attorney's Evidence of the Baptism of the Holy Spirit (Los Angeles: Full Gospel Businessmen's Fellowship, Inc., n.d.). These booklets contain the testimonies of persons in these professions and how "The Baptism of the Holy Spirit" helped them to do their work better."

[46]From Doctrinal Statement of FGBMFI.

[47]Respondent No. 97.

[48]Respondent No. 71.

[49]Glock, op. cit., p. 212.

[50]Bob Jones, "God in Government," Voice 21:7 (July-August, 1973), p. 28.

[51]Peter Berger, The Sacred Canopy (New York: Double-day Anchor Book, 1967); see also J. Milton Yinger, The Scientific Study of Religion (New York: Macmillan, 1970), p. 21.

[52]Glock, op. cit.

[53]Respondent No. 41.

[54]Respondent No. 1.

[55]Respondent No. 38.

[56]Respondent No. 71.

[57]Respondent No. 96.

[58]Respondent No. 19.

[59]This is a common theme in most testimonies.

[60]Respondent No. 3.

[61]Robert K. Merton, "Social Structure and Anomie," Social Theory and Social Structure (New York: The Free Press, 1968), pp. 185-214.

[62]Respondent No. 1.

[63]John Kildahl, The Psychology of Speaking in Tongues (New York: Harper and Row, Inc., 1972) pp. 63-64.

[64]Respondent No. 5.

[65]Thomas F. O'Dea, The Sociology of Religion (Englewood Cliffs, New Jersey: Prentice Hall, Inc., 1966) p. 15.

[66]Respondent No. 3.

[67]Respondent No. 9.

[68]Respondent No. 2.

[69]Henry W. Baxter, Jr., "Out of the Shadows," Voice 21:11 (December, 1973), pp. 14-19.

[70]Arnold W. Green, _Sociology_ (New York: McGraw Hill, 1956), p. 546.

[71]Respondent No. 9.

[72]Respondent No. 105.

[73]Respondent No. 66.

[74]Respondent No. 7.

[75]Respondent No. 7.

[76]Bryan Wilson, "Sects and Society," _Studies in British Society_, ed. J. A. Banks (New York: Thomas Y. Crowell Co., 1968), p. 72.

[77]Dean Kelly, _Why Conservative Churches are Growing_ (New York: Harper and Row, 1972), pp. 24-27.

[78]Glock, _op. cit._, p. 211.

[79]Respondent No. 7.

[80]Respondent No. 1.

[81]Respondent No. 86.

[82]Andrew Greeley, _Ecstasy: A Way of Knowing_ (Englewood Cliffs, New Jersey: Prentice Hall, 1974), p. 11.

[83]Gerlach and Hine, _op. cit._, pp. 23-40.

Chapter III

[1]Bryan Wilson, _Religious Sects_ (New York: McGraw Hill, 1970).

[2]Liston Pope, _Millhands and Preachers_ (New Haven: Yale University Press, 1942).

[3]Respondent No. 5.

[4]Thomas F. O'Dea, "Anomie and the Quest for Community: The Formation of Sects Among Puerto Ricans of New York," _American Catholic Sociological Review_ 21 (Spring, 1960), pp. 18-36.

[5]David Riessman, Nathan Glazer, and Reuel Denney, _The Lonely Crowd: A Study in the Changing American Character_ (New Haven: Yale University Press, 1961), pp. 246-259.

[6]Will Herberg, _Protestant, Catholic, Jew_ (Garden City, New Jersey: Doubleday and Company, 1955).

[7]Ferdinand Tonnies, _Fundamental Concepts of Sociology_, trans. Charles Loomis (New York: McGraw-Hill, 1940), p. 40.

[8]Respondent No. 50.

[9]L. P. Gerlach and V. H. Hine, "Five Factors Crucial to the Growth and Spread of a Modern Religious Movement," _Journal for the Scientific Study of Religion_ 7 (Spring, 1968), pp. 23-40.

ABOUT THE AUTHOR

Cecil David Bradfield earned his Ph.D. in sociology from The American University and holds Masters degrees in social science and theology from James Madison University and Trinity Lutheran Seminary. His B.A. in social science was earned at Capital University in Columbus, Ohio.

Dr. Bradfield is currently Associate Professor of Sociology at James Madison University and has contributed articles to journals in sociology and related fields. He has also been a frequent presenter at professional meetings as well as a consultant to religious organizations. Prior to his coming to James Madison University, Dr. Bradfield served as a Lutheran Pastor in Eastern West Virginia.

The author is married to the former Nancy Rexrode and is the father of one child, Anne Cecilia.